The Dog Stays
in the Picture

The Dog Stays in the Picture

Life Lessons from a Rescued Greyhound

SUSAN MORSE

OPEN ROAD

INTEGRATED MEDIA

NEW YORK

Copyright © 2014 by Susan Morse

Cover design by Andrea Worthington

Cover photograph by Boprey Photography

978-1-4976-4393-2

Published in 2014 by Open Road Integrated Media, Inc.
345 Hudson Street
New York, NY 10014
www.openroadmedia.com

For David.
And Lilly.

Contents

Author's Note   3

1. What If   5
2. The Talisman   14
3. Fever   34
4. Lilly [sic]   47
5. Nothing Is Broken   55
6. *Toy Story*   81
7. Releasing   94
8. Sleep Disorder   108
9. The SBDs   118
10. Anatidaephobia   143
11. Fossils and Quacks   155

CONTENTS

12. Coincidence?   183

13. Breakthrough   206

14. Bookends   216

15. Front-Hall Bridge   228

A Note on Greyhound Adoption   247

Acknowledgments   249

Photo Credits   251

About the Author   253

The Dog Stays
in the Picture

Author's Note

This is not a book about a dog.
I really do prefer my husband—honest.
But it's hard to tell the story of our journey into the empty nest,
and leave out one particular animal.
Which kind of illustrates the problem.

1.

What If

Life after children was going to be magic.

Curtain up: A swank hotel ~~room~~ *suite in* ~~London Paris Venice~~ *Dubai. Shades are drawn, lights dimmed. Faint soundtrack of mellow jazz. David (mid-fifties, handsome and well-built but with heart-melting character) is shirtless, reclining on the plush, king-size bed, glancing over a scene for work* ~~tomorrow morning at six a.m.~~ *next week sometime. He has lit a candle.*

Susan (early fifties, but with the body of a ~~sixteen-~~ ~~twenty-nine-~~ ~~thirty-five-~~ *reasonably well-preserved middle-aged woman) emerges from the bathroom* ~~naked~~ *wearing a negligee. She stalks to the bed jungle-she-cat-style, slithers under the sheets, and glowers pointedly at David.*

5

David ~~keeps reading for like an hour~~ drops his script immediately, flips Susan on her back, and has at it.

SUSAN. *(Up for air)* Okay. Now: say that thing you always said in that movie in North Carolina.

DAVID. What thing? Which movie?

SUSAN. You know. You were the big redneck with the long straggly hair and the muscles straining through the dirty wife-beater and you pushed Robin Wright up against the wall and after you got brain damage you were always saying—

DAVID. *(Growling)* Yes ma'am?

SUSAN. That's it! Say it!

DAVID. *(Breathing in her ear)* Yes ma'am, yes, oh yes ma'am.

SUSAN. Okay now you can stop saying it.

They writhe. Curtain down.

I really thought we'd earned Dubai. We're a show-business anomaly—married almost thirty years, although technically we've been together only half that time, if you factor in all the long stretches apart while David was on location and I was at home keeping things normal for our three little ones. Now the first of those little ones, Eliza, our eldest, is already at college, and the last two (twin sons Ben and Sam) are high school seniors in the process of applying. Soon there will be nothing to keep David and me apart—except for my fixation on a certain new animal. Someone should have stopped me.

David didn't try to intervene when I chose this dog. He's still kind of in trouble for something he did back when the children were small. Many years ago, my husband went away for a while and fell violently in love:

—*She's perfect, Susan.*

—*Excuse me?*

—*She is extremely intelligent and sweet. I want her to live with us.*

—*David, I am pretty sure I—*

—*You'll be fine. She's perfect. The kids will be thrilled.*

—*David, I wish I had time to explain to you how difficult this would be for me, but—oh no, hold the phone a second—BEN! NO! These are NOT CANDY, Ben, we DON'T EAT them. They're lightbulbs, YUCKY. Sorry David, what were you—OH my GOSH I think I smell SMOKE—*

—*She won't be any trouble, Susan, I promise. And when I do the play, I can take her to New York. I get so lonely without you.*

My husband has always been the trustworthy sort. He's worked with the big boys from time to time, and there are usually babes around the big boys, eager for their chance. According to David, when things don't go their way, these babes inevitably seek comfort by offering themselves rather boldly to the second male lead. This has to be tempting if your family is thousands of miles away, but so far David has always come home.

I've tried not to let the situation stress me. There's nothing I can do about it, and anyway the kids have always kept me too busy to think past the next minute. I wasn't really buying David's promise to keep his intelligent new friend out of my hair—how was he going to take care of a *dog* while working sixteen-hour days in some strange city? Eliza was ten and Ben and Sam were starting first grade, which meant for the first time in a decade I'd have weekdays all to myself, and I had plans for those weekdays that did not include helping a new animal adjust to our household, no matter how sweet she might be. So I laid down the law and when David came home alone the following week I believed the subject was closed. Then, while he was unpacking, Sam and Ben came down to the kitchen brandishing one of those little quickie Fotomat albums.

—*She's so cute, Mama! These people can't keep her anymore and she's about to be homeless! We have to have her. They told Papa her name means "clown" in French!*

Her name was Perro, which immediately got my French Lit major knickers bunched.

—*"Perro" is a Spanish word, meaning "dog," not "clown." If whoever named this dog intended to call her "clown" in French, they forgot to check their French-English dictionary.*

—*The French word for clown is actually "pierrot,"* I informed David, stressing the guttural "rr" in the back of my throat. *And besides, if she's female, that name is completely inaccurate. It should be Pierr-ETTE. Pierr-OT, even when pronounced properly, is a MALE clown.*

—*We can call her Pierrette, Susan. Anything you like. You're going to LOVE her.*

David's uncharacteristic, absolute insistence puzzled me. *Midlife crisis?* I wondered. I decided it was best to cooperate, even if I knew this wannabe French intruder was not likely to work out as David's traveling companion and I'd get stuck at home with her. Perhaps my sacrifice could serve as a sort of guilt-propelled inoculation against any lurking babes. So Perro was delivered, and she became Arrow, because Arrow sort of rhymed.

We are dog-and-cat people. We've always had at least one of each. Arrow overlapped for a few years with our first dog, Aya, elderly by then, an Australian shepherd mutt, who eventually taught Arrow most of the ropes. It took me some time to get a handle on Arrow's appalling leash manners and her various transgressions (gnawing through the furniture in the TV room—the kids, those wretches, sprawled beside her, oblivious), but her sweet eagerness to please wore me down, and finally I had to admit David knew how to spot a good dog. Arrow turned out to be perfect for us—a lovely, unforgettable animal, part shepherd like Aya, but mostly a hunter—and her best friend was Joey, our cat. Joey was Robin to Arrow's Batman. Both black-and-white, and thick as thieves; they had chipmunk flushing down to a science.

Joey and Arrow

Until, as these things go, Arrow was wrenched from us last spring at age twelve. Too soon. One minute she was racing up and down the fence line, advising passersby of their rights, and the next she had no appetite—an inoperable, football-sized tumor in her abdomen. We grieved long and hard (even I did), sprinkled her ashes on a favorite, secret island off the coast of Maine, and then, in the fall, with the boys starting college applications, with Dubai just around the corner, it was my turn to pick the dog.

What we have here is a cautionary tale.

Maybe I sabotaged us because I was too anxious about the upcoming childless chapter in our marriage to risk changing the status quo. I was the youngest and last child to leave my parents' nest, and they did not settle into a new, happier life. When I was finally at boarding school, my father sent his family antiques to auction in order to pay off mounting debts, moved out to drink in peace in a pay-by-the-week hotel, and had a non-fatal heart attack. My mother yelled on the phone a lot, had a long and colorful nervous breakdown in the old, empty, six-bedroom house of my childhood, and took in boarders.

David's father left the nest even before any kids did, so there is legitimate cause for concern about our own situation. I worry how David will cope, having to spend his golden years with a brain-frizzled zombie who has not done much lately but drive children back and forth to school and struggle around the block with the dog. After the 1994 earthquake in Northridge, California, when we moved the family east and faced the fact that I should quit acting to focus on our children, I began wondering what exactly my life would amount to. Friends are quick to remind me that stay-at-home mothers *do* have real, vital jobs, and are perfectly intelligent, interesting, productive, and valuable people. Still, I'd toss at night, contemplating my lame obituary:

Susan Wheeler Duff von Moschzisker Morse went to blah college and acted in a few movies, plays, and television series. She taught horseback riding to underprivileged children. Then she edited some books. She was mostly kind to pets, and tried to keep the plants watered.

She is survived by her mother (who will never die); her three children, Eliza, Benjamin, and Samuel Morse; and her husband, actor David Morse, who is the truly interesting person in the family, so why don't we stop bothering to dredge up things to say about Susan and skip to the good stuff?

David Morse has played more men in uniform than you can shake a stick at, and will be fondly remembered as the death row prison guard who got a face-full of chewed-up Moon Pie spat at him by Sam Rockwell, who was having (come to think of it) his own breakthrough performance as a rebellious inmate, in The Green Mile, *starring mainly Tom Hanks.*

Actually, let's drop the Morses and Sam Rockwell altogether and focus on what's newsworthy: the long and venerable Oscar-winning career of Mr. Hanks. Tom is married to actress Rita Wilson. Now THERE'S a feisty woman with REAL backbone! Rita Wilson's hus-

band travels a lot too, and Rita has children AND a career. She acts!
She produces movies! Rita probably lets Tom have JILLIONS of dogs!

Betty Friedan's *The Feminine Mystique* offered novel food for
thought to stay-at-home mothers in the early '60s: If you embrace
this homemaker lifestyle, wrote Friedan, don't think of it as a dead
end. Get ready, because once the children grow up, you *can* go out
into the world and *do* something. You really can! And I know this is
possible. My parents patched things up eventually, and redefined
themselves in surprising ways well into old age. When they retired
together to Florida, my ex-lawyer father hosted a cable talk show
and dabbled in acting. He peaked as the priest conducting a funeral
in *Dead Poets Society*—Daddy had no lines and they cut most of
his scene, but he died fulfilled. After he was gone, my eighty-five-
year-old mother raised the bar further by transforming herself
into Mother Brigid, an Orthodox Christian nun. My parents have
been something other than dull.

But married life after children is a crapshoot no matter what,
and I get a little anxious when I hear of couple after couple splitting up when their kids are gone. For a long time, I've been batting
away horror fantasies, the flip side of Dubai:

Curtain up: A creaky front hallway of an old haunted-type house.
Tumbleweeds tumble forlornly past a dog, Arrow (lying flat and
motionless in a cobweb-covered travel crate next to a pile of molder-
ing suitcases).

Susan (garish, troweled-on Norma Desmond makeup; indeterminate Miss Havisham–age category) drifts in, dialing a cordless phone. A faded-blue, no-longer-slinky ball gown she wore decades ago in her TV debut on ABC's The Fall Guy *hangs pathetically from her hunched crone shoulders, its long, tattered train dragging an eerie serpentine channel in the dust-caked floor. Susan looks down at Arrow.*

SUSAN. Arrow, did you hear the doorbell?

(Arrow, taxidermied as a perpetual reminder to David, cannot respond.)

SUSAN. Hello, is this *Celebrity Wives' Car Service?* This is Susan Morse and my car is awfully late. I've been waiting almost *(checks watch)* thirty years for you to take the dog and me to the airport so we can join my husband, David, on location in ~~Dublin~~ ~~Reykjavik~~ ~~Toronto~~ um, I think it's somewhere in Kansas, which is better than nothing . . . What? You just dropped us all off at our apartment in New York? *What* apartment in New York? That's not *me* who's with him— who the heck is it? Wait, what kind of dog do they have? Never mind, I don't want to know. Just go back and tell him I'm still here, the *first* wife, with the *original* dog. We are waiting, and the dog is *not* taking this well.

Curtain down.

2.

The Talisman

It's amazing how certain inanimate objects take on an emotional charge. Dog-eared books, heirloom Christmas decorations, and framed pictures are practically designed for sentimentality. But I'm more struck by the unlikely ones. There's this utilitarian item at the foot of our cellar stairs: a small, unremarkable, individual-sized Little Playmate by Igloo cooler. The rest of the family hardly seems aware the Little Playmate is there. To me, it radiates protection, like a talisman. I can't pass it these days without a lump forming in my throat. Loading up the car with Eliza's college things at the end of recent summers, I've considered making room for it.

THE DOG STAYS IN THE PICTURE

*   *   *

A few days after she was born, Eliza turned yellow. The doctor diagnosed jaundice, caused by an excess of bilirubin in the bloodstream. This is supposedly nothing to worry about. It can happen when a newborn's liver hasn't had a chance to get fully up and running, and it's not hard to fix.

We were instructed to feed the baby more often, keep a detailed log describing the color and consistency of the contents of every diaper, and give her plenty of nude sunbaths. They sent a nurse to install a huge, intimidating "bili light" over Eliza's crib, and gave us tiny eyeshades to protect her little blue eyes during phototherapy treatments.

Eliza was our first, and I couldn't believe we were being trusted to fix the situation *ourselves*. I kept compulsively poking her forehead to see if the skin still looked yellow where I pressed. This little person I'd fallen head over heels in love with was utterly dependent on us and it scared me.

One morning David found me distraught in the gliding rocker chair, blubbering over our sleeping saffron-hued daughter, and asked what was the matter.

—*She's so* limp!

—*Aren't they supposed to be limp at this stage?*

—*Yes, but David, she needs us so much and we have to take care of her!*

—*Well, we* are, *Susan*—

—*I know, I know we are, now, but the thing is we can't take care of her forever! It's killing me!*

—*Susan, I don't think—you do understand at some point Eliza's going to want her own life.*

—*I know, and that's okay, really, Eliza can have her own life. All I want is for her to be happy, so of course she should live her own life and do whatever she wants.*

—*So what's the matter?*

—*Oh, I just can't bear it! What about when she's had her long, happy life, and she's suddenly old, and all vulnerable again? Where will we be then, when she's limp and helpless? Nowhere!*

—*Susan.*

—*She'll be all alone, and we have no idea whatsoever who's going to be there to hold her and feed her! Who's going to care if Eliza's poops are the right color? Nobody!*

—*Susan.*

—*Oh my gosh, are you laughing?*

—*No.*

—*You are!*

—*Susan, I swear I'm not laughing.*

—*Stop it! This is serious, David! We've gone and made this amazing, beautiful person who is our responsibility and there is nothing we'll be able to do when she really needs us, because we'll be dead!*

I have an actress friend who's extremely good at weeping on cue. She uses a photo of her favorite dog, now deceased, if she needs to cry for the camera. If I were still acting now, I know what I'd try: I'd pull out my iPod, stick in the ear buds, and play one track from the London Cast Recording of *Les Misérables,* because Patti LuPone's defining interpretation of the simple song "Fantine's Death" gets me every time. I used to listen to it obsessively.

Fantine has had to resort to prostitution to support her illegitimate child. She dies of tuberculosis in the middle of the first act, but not before singing a couple of major showstoppers, and especially not before making sure Jean Valjean promises at Fantine's deathbed to look after her young, fatherless daughter, Cosette, who is living with the mean innkeeper and his wife.

In "Fantine's Death," Fantine is in her hovel, fading in and out of a fevered hallucinatory fantasy in which she thinks she is tenderly readying her absent daughter for bed, surfacing occasionally, just long enough to confirm custody arrangements, such as they are, with Valjean. By this point in the song, I'm usually in a state of perverse ecstasy—agonized maternal bliss. I have learned I can't play this music in the car—I could easily forget myself and run into a telephone pole.

We lived in Los Angeles until Eliza was in her last year of Montessori preschool. Her first year, they suggested we *put together an earthquake kit for your child to keep in the classroom,* so I filled our Little Playmate by Igloo cooler with provisions, and went over everything with my friend Susan who, like me with the twins, was nursing a newborn. The recommended list made me

17

feel a little faint, and Susan had a sudden spontaneous breast-milk letdown.

- *Water* (Oh my gosh, how many days' worth?)
- *Band-Aids* (Exactly what good are Band-Aids going to do her if she breaks a leg or splits her head open? How about some plasma and a splint?)
- *A flashlight* (Yes. Thank you.)
- *Nonperishable comfort food, like granola bars and raisins* (Sorry, but all Eliza will eat right now is pancakes. May I throw in my special mix?)
- *A small cuddly toy* (Jeez. Can we please change the subject?)
- *A photo of parents, and a card with the name and phone number of relatives or friends living out of state* (Got it. Meaning anyone living safely away from the fault line. Meaning still alive. In case her parents are *not*. Okay. How about I just die right now and get it over with.)

As it turned out, we did have a big earthquake in L.A., but Eliza did not need her Little Playmate by Igloo because we were all at home asleep when it hit. Eliza was five and her brothers were barely two. Ben was getting over pneumonia, which I was beginning to think I might be catching, so I had decided to try knocking it out with a good night's sleep in our sub-ground guest room, accessed by its own separate entrance from the back patio, below the kitchen.

We'd been living in L.A. for over a decade, and occasional earth tremors did not really faze us. If my extended family fretted about the possibility of disaster, I'd use the old comeback, *We're more likely to get hit by a car on the freeway than killed in an earthquake.* In the night we'd sometimes wake up, our bedposts rattling from a little shudder, and I'd think, *We can either get up and find out what's going on, or go back to sleep. Either way, if we're going to die, we're going to die.* That had been my careless attitude BC (meaning "before children").

They tell you the worst place to be in an earthquake is on the bottom level of a house, for obvious reasons. The night the big one hit I woke abruptly in my guest-room quarantine zone under the kitchen to a real nightmare—walls cracking behind my headboard; plaster speckling the quilt. A monster truck was driving through the kitchen overhead, and I did not roll over and resign myself to death or even take a second to think. I shot out the door onto the patio in the pitch-dark.

It took a few seconds to get my bearings. House alarms and car sirens were echoing through the San Fernando Valley. The patio was bucking under my feet like a ceramic trampoline, and I sort of staggered in circles trying to stay upright while the beautiful Mediterranean tiles we'd installed on our roof a couple of years before plummeted down around me from three stories up, smashing left and right.

I was focused completely on my family upstairs in the house. I knew the first thing to do in a situation this extreme is to immediately—DO NOT PASS GO—shut off the gas supply in case of a leak, so the house won't blow up. In this particular situation, because I was closest, gas shutoff was definitely my job.

Our valve was in the front yard. Shutting it off required a wrench, which we kept (as instructed) right by the valve for just this kind of emergency. But lately the boys had been toddling around out there—they were obsessed with that wrench—so when I blundered along the side path and out the gate to the front and scrabbled around for it in the dark—no wrench.

I let myself in the front door to find the spare. We kept a tool-box in our garage, which was all the way at the other end of the house. Our burglar alarm has voice commands, and the backup battery must have kicked in because the buzzer was going, and a robot man's voice was coming out of all the alarm panels. *(Front. Door: Open. Of-fice. Win-dow: Open. Bal-cony. Door: Open.)* It was about four thirty a.m. and pretty dark, but I could tell a lot of pictures had fallen on the floor, and there was quite a bit of broken glass. I will never understand why I didn't cut my bare feet that night, but I managed to crunch safely over everything to reach the bottom of the stairs and call to David:

—*David?*

—*Yes!*

—*Is everyone all right?*

—*Yes! Are you?*

—*Oh, thank God! Yes! I'm going to get the wrench to shut off the gas.*

—*Good girl!*

I have never forgotten that exchange. It meant the world to me.

The story from David's side was quite something. He was fast asleep when a freight-train sound came booming across the valley. He had no clothes on, and when the shaking reached our house and the beams of our four-poster began to rattle, he leapt into action, still partly asleep. The floor was bucking under him the same way the patio had for me, so he couldn't get his footing and skinned his knees on the carpet, then made a dash for the boys' room, running straight into our new live-in nanny, Yolanda, who was coming out of Eliza's bedroom across the hall.

Sometime after the twins were born, sleep deprivation raised legitimate safety concerns. Yolanda began helping us part-time, and we had only just asked her to move in permanently. This was her first official night. She was in the country on a work visa from El Salvador, which has had its share of deadly earthquakes, so this was not Yolanda's first, nor was it the worst she'd been through. She kept her cool like a true veteran—didn't even bat an eye at David's lack of clothing.

When David got to the boys' room, Ben was standing in his crib. Knowing one child was alive, David asked Yolanda to grab Ben so he could get Sam, who was in the other crib, motionless, almost stiff, under a heavy dusting of plaster. This is when David remembered with a jolt why Yolanda had been sleeping in Eliza's room—Eliza, going through a needy stage, was currently spending her nights with us in the master bedroom on a little pallet at the foot of our bed. So David tucked Sam under one arm and sprinted back for

Eliza, ignoring Yolanda's pleas. *(Go find Mrs. Susan, Mr. David. I'll stay with the niños.)* There were three children to deal with, and anyway what could he do for me, two floors down under the house?

In our bedroom, the alarm clock had landed on the floor and was blaring, along with Robot Alarm Man. *(Bed-room. Win-dow: Open.)* Eliza was very still, on her pallet, also covered in plaster. A large painting and a lamp were piled on top of her, but miraculously, like Sam, she too was asleep and, still holding Sam, David somehow pulled her out from under everything.

With one child under each arm, David then stationed himself on the floor in the master-bedroom doorway. (We were told a doorway is the safest place. It worked out okay that night but it's actually not such a good idea, we learned recently from an earthquake forensics expert. Doorways are weak. The best place to be, if possible, is tucked on the floor next to a large sturdy piece of furniture, like a desk or bureau—*next* to it, not *under* or you could get squished depending on how heavy the beams are when they come down. If you're tight up against something solid, when the ceiling beams come down they'll be more likely to tilt on landing, forming a triangle, and you'll be inside a safe little pocket of protected space.)

This was the scene when I called up the stairs about finding a wrench for the gas: Naked David with plaster-coated Eliza and Sam sitting in the doorway to our bedroom; Yolanda and Ben in the boys' doorway across the hall. (Yolanda praying *Santa María, Madre de Dios . . .*)

—David?

—Yes!

—Is everyone all right?

—Yes! Are you?

—Oh, thank God! Yes!

I love reliving that moment.

Because our house was deemed unlivable by the inspectors, we camped at a friend's for a time, and subsequently moved to Philadelphia. David was beginning Sean Penn's movie *The Crossing Guard*, a big break and an extremely challenging part, and he felt he'd worry too much if we stayed in California. He wanted us off the fault line permanently, and I agreed. Those few adrenaline-shot laps around the patio in the dark with sirens blasting and tiles raining down were my moment of truth. The kids, and safety, would always come first.

Our dog and cat had to deal for a while. I'd like to say we knew we could count on their inborn self-preservation instinct to get through, but the truth is we were in shock, with three little children to protect, and nobody can actually remember thinking about the animals during the earthquake and its aftershocks. I am so grateful we never had to face the awful *Sophie's Choice* decision some Katrina survivors did, trapped on their rooftops, contemplating a rescue boat that could not accommodate anything besides humans.

It took the kids, Yolanda, and me months to settle back east before we could send for Aya and Marbles, a recently rescued kitten still in recovery from her own singularly Dickensian early life before the earthquake. We stayed with many kind friends and relatives, and everywhere we went, Ben and Sam managed to locate a couple of wrenchlike objects first thing, and they'd march around brandishing them, sternly repeating, *Gotta turn off da GAS, Mama!*

The series of moves was particularly discombobulating for Eliza. In Philadelphia I tried settling her in a local Montessori school run by the Saint Joseph nuns, who promised an appealing mission of caring for the "Whole Family" in their brochure, and I found a posttraumatic-stress-type family therapist for support. It was rough going—Eliza was quite out of sorts, and I wasn't sure how to help.

One afternoon I left her sleeping in the car for a few seconds while I brought in the groceries. We were house-sitting at a home with a long driveway, sheltered from the street in a peaceful neighborhood. It was toward the end of a cold February; snow was still on the ground even though the day was sunny and the temperature seemed okay. (So I thought. I had not yet got the hang of things on the East Coast.)

When I went into the house, the phone rang. While I was answering I looked out the window to make sure Eliza was all right, and had to drop everything and make a dash for it. Eliza had woken up, the car was heating in the sun more quickly than I'd anticipated, and she was panicked, sobbing, and hyperventilating in the backseat.

Eliza was unusually clingy at school drop-offs after that, and I had an unhelpful tendency to linger till she was happy. The PTSD therapist instructed me to stay very calm, matter-of-fact, and not to be overly demonstrative when saying good-bye. This behavior did not come naturally to me. I really felt Eliza's pain, and wanted nothing more than to scoop her up and take her home with me. But I tried to be stoic, and Eliza's sweet, gentle teacher would watch us at the door, perplexed: Eliza begging me not to go, and me with my poker face, forcing out awkward reassurance, Robot Alarm Man–style. *(You will be. O-kay. I'll be back. Ve-ry soon.)*

I don't think it was only earthquake trauma that made me so desperately attached to Eliza; it just made things more complicated. I'd been this way since her jaundice, and when I'd wrestled myself away and shut that schoolroom door I'd go home with an uneasy feeling. There was something about the look on that teacher's face. . . .

David was still filming in L.A. Yolanda had agreed to come with us and help out in Philadelphia, and she and the boys were getting along famously. I was making a special effort to give our traumatized daughter as much quality time as possible, and so we went to her school's Family Fun Day, just the two of us.

Eliza and I were sitting with our juice boxes on a little patch of grass, watching jolly children and their parents walking by. Out of nowhere this stern old nun I had never laid eyes on before stopped and said: *Hello, Eliza.*

Eliza did not seem to know who this was, and I smiled. But the nun did not make eye contact with me at all, and disappeared into the crowd. That uneasy feeling again.

We'd moved to yet another post-earthquake temporary rental, a vintage *Addams Family*–style gabled Victorian, which usually served as our church's rectory, and David came home from filming. One afternoon a friend brought her three children over for an afternoon playdate, and the house was busy. At some point I happened to glance out a leaded front window, and paused to watch a sort of ordinary man with a clipboard ease tentatively out of his car and linger at the end of our front walk, gazing up at the façade. Jehovah's Witness, maybe? He seemed to be psyching himself up in exactly the way that banker with the briefcase used to screw up his courage before knocking on the Addams Family's front door. Long story short: it was Child Protective Services.

This was about the car episode. Eliza explained to me later that she had felt she needed a hug one day at school. She figured out she could have one if she told her teacher she was upset because her mother had left her in the car alone and it got really hot and she was sooo scared.

Ever since Eliza's outpouring, behind the scenes, her teacher began watching my weird Robot Mama routine at drop-off and scanned Eliza daily for possible bruises. She had mentioned something about Eliza's car story in a conference I'd requested, but it didn't occur to naïve me (or to the teacher, as she explained when I later called in a panic after Mr. Child Protector's visit) that the headmistress (the creepy old nun from Family Fun Day!) had decided to alert the state.

So now we had a new kind of danger to grapple with. This

was my hometown—people knew me, sort of. But I was returning after more than a decade, with a new exotic identity: Wife of Movie Actor. Kurt Cobain had just died, and his wife, Courtney Love, was battling rumors of heroin addiction and trying to keep custody of their new baby. David and I were not interesting enough for the tabloids and never would be (thank God). But he was playing an ex-con in *The Crossing Guard*. David prepares for his roles meticulously, so he had this fantastic new hard-earned prison-yard bodybuilder physique; he had grown his hair long and was keeping it slicked back in a greasy little ponytail; and whenever he turned up in our small, cloistered new neighborhood, people did not quite know what to make of him. Our family portrait was not looking exactly suburban.

David, Eliza, Sam, and Ben, 1994

Here the children were, just recovering from a natural disaster, supposedly safe, only to be possibly ripped from their parents and dumped in *foster care*?!

Mr. Child Protector turned out to be extremely good at his job, thank goodness. He talked to me and David, sniffed around our house a little, and took a few minutes alone with Eliza. Then he told us this was the most pleasant assignment he'd ever had (it was quite a novelty to evaluate a wholesome family for once, he said), and our slate was wiped clean as if nothing had ever happened.

I ran into Eliza's old teacher at the market some years later. We had a good talk, and I told her Eliza was happy in her new school, much more settled. She said things were a lot better for her students, too—they had replaced that creepy nun, their headmistress.

The first weekend I ever dared leave our kids was the following year. David had been nominated for an award for *The Crossing Guard*, and the producers flew me out to meet him in L.A. for the ceremony. I lined up the children's favorite, most responsible sitter, an assistant DA paying off law school. Eliza had a really hard time going to bed the night before I left, so we did not get much sleep, and I was in a bit of a daze getting on the plane. There was heavy turbulence midflight—long periods of shaking, the hammering kind where lights flicker and flight attendants take to their seats. Like the improbable threat of earthquakes, turbulence BC had never bothered me much. But on that first solo flight since the kids were born, I sort of snapped: *Who will take care of them if I crash?*

I know you're not in any real danger in turbulence, but I simply could not get it together—*Okay, so I'm not going to crash but what about the next time I have to fly with the kids and we have bumps like this and they are a little scared? What if I make it even worse because I am freaking out myself? We'll never be able to visit David on location, the children will not have a relationship with their father, and he will divorce me because we never see each other, and basically the world as we know it is going to end because I can't keep collected on a bumpy flight!*

I was so desperate I picked up the air phone under my tray table and called my mother, of all people. For once, I did not object when she suggested we recite the Lord's Prayer together. (The woman sitting beside me, who did not seem even slightly alarmed by the bumping, acted as if nothing was happening.)

I am not a prescription-drug-type person, but since then I've always flown with anxiety meds. They work! When the bumps start, all I am aware of is distant muffled screams—a lunatic lady locked in some secret, padded compartment deep inside my psyche, screeching and wailing. I feel completely at ease. I just smile sympathetically and think, *Poor woman. So glad that's not me.*

Another item I'd definitely have in my iPod for help with those acting preparations: the soundtrack of *Mamma Mia!*

This is very serious stuff. I am about one-quarter Swedish, and I should know. Those ABBA Swedes have soul.

Halfway through middle school I finally began to believe that Eliza had truly found her independence. The penny drop may have had something to do with the difference in protocol between lower and middle school. In lower school you could walk your child into homeroom, and most people did. Since homeroom drop-off was an option, there was no question: I was of course going to park the car and go in with my daughter. (If sitting in the classroom breast-feeding your eight-year-old on your lap all day had been an option, I would have seen it as my duty.) I never did get the hang of that lower-school drop-off technique, so when David was at home, that was his job, and he was a lot better than I was at separating calmly with Eliza in the mornings. I dropped the boys off. The boys did not give a rat's ass *who* dropped them off, or even where. They had each other, so there was never an issue. Maybe God saw how badly I was muffing it with Eliza and gave us twins to save everyone a little stress.

By middle school, with the help of wonderful Ms. Tinari and Ms. Ferguson in their full-length down coats, smiling and dancing from one foot to another for warmth at the frosty curb every morning, Eliza and I finally learned to release with dignity. Eliza would hop out and trot gaily up the steps. I would be okay, I guessed. By the end of eighth grade I'd only occasionally linger to watch her pink backpack disappear through the glass doors before I'd well up, and have to gulp it back on my way up the driveway. *She's growing up fast. . . .*

By the spring of that last middle-school year she had a boy-friend. Eliza was thirteen, and being seen places with her mother was becoming a bit of an embarrassment. But she was forced into my company one evening in order to satisfy a requirement: Eliza had to attend a music concert of some kind, and write a paper about it. A Broadway musical seemed like the least painful outing, and the only touring company in Philly that spring was *Mamma Mia!*

We knew nothing about it. I had totally missed ABBA in the '70s, but my sister Colette, who is British and very cutting-edge, claims that their harmony is on the level with Bach or something crazy like that, and their material can be surprisingly primal, as well. For the uninitiated: ABBA was made up of two married couples. The name is a sort of anagram because both women's names begin with an "A" and the men's begin with a "B." When the first "AB" pair divorced, they managed to keep the group together for a while. Some of the songs they wrote and performed toward the end were intensely personal, illustrations of the turmoil they were going through in their relationships: Picture A, belting out her anguish over B's infidelity, while B, who actually wrote the song, is onstage playing backup. I was intrigued.

During the first act, I think Eliza was too cool for school, attitude-wise, and to be honest, I was as well. I wanted to keep my mind open, but we both felt out of our element and were having a sort of reverse mother-daughter bonding experience, both of us rolling our eyes at all the screaming middle-aged women around us leaping to their feet for the climactic dance numbers. *Platform shoes and glitter Spandex!* So I was not expecting to be blindsided in Act II. There's a heartfelt, simple ballad, "Slipping Through My Fingers," where the central character (the

Mamma) is helping her daughter into her wedding dress, reminiscing about how it felt to watch her "funny little girl" leave home with her schoolbag in the early morning.

Sitting in the dark, surrounded by sniffling menopausal women, next to my own funny little girl on the eve of high school *(The driver's license! The college applications!)*, the song ripped me right out of my snarky attitude into a deep place; I was jettisoned instantly back to my minivan in the school drop-off lane, watching that pink backpack bob eagerly up the steps. Tears streaming, nose running, all the while desperately keeping my head as low as possible, trying to conceal my sudden ABBA conversion from Eliza, because if she realized I'd been sucked in like this she would either be mortified, or worse, fall apart herself.

I am beginning to sense I'm not the only hysterical helicopter in the box. I have company—my friend Susan, with her earthquake-kit milk letdown, for one, and these ABBA ladies, with their hot flashes, whimpering next to me in the dark. I really felt a connection with the ABBA ladies that night, and if Eliza hadn't been there I probably would have joined the Conga line they formed up and down the aisles of the Shubert Theatre for the grand finale. *(Waterloo!!!)* And then I'd have taken these new sisters of mine out for coffee and asked the million-dollar question: What's this primal thing that bonds us to our kids? And what's the shift we're making—this shift from worrying we'll die and leave our children defenseless, to despairing because they're not going to need us anymore?

Seven years after the earthquake, we finally summoned the nerve to buy a house here in Philadelphia. We held out until we could afford something East Coast old—sturdy, with plenty of space—and somehow the Little Playmate by Igloo earthquake cooler made it across the country to our unfinished cellar. Flashlights and homemade pancake mix are no longer an issue, but David sometimes uses it to transport ice packs to work when he has to run all day or punch some people. Mostly, the Little Playmate sits unnoticed at the bottom of the stairs, waiting to be needed, a talisman. You can still make out my handwriting in faded black Sharpie on the wrinkled sticker:

3.

Fever

I wish I could bring the kids on board.

—Why can't we get another mutt, Mama? Greyhounds are snotty-looking.

—That is so not true, Ben. This is not about buying a fancy purebred. This is still rescue, but on a much larger scale than we're used to. I've been reading up. They say these dogs have lived entirely in crates, with numbers tattooed inside their ears, and track people kill them when they can't race. They toss them on the trash heap! They're like canine refugees.

—They need too much exercise. You'll have to run it all the time or it will drive everyone crazy.

—Also not true. The O'Briens' greyhounds have a walk once a day, and the rest of the time they just lie there.

—Well. It's not my type of dog. But go ahead if you want to.

The subtext being: *I'm leaving soon anyway.*

My passion started decades ago at the Philadelphia Kennel Club show in Center City, where I saw my first Afghan hounds: glam, limber, wide-eyed, toothy *Charlie's Angels*–era Farrah Fawcett stunners, shag hairstyles fluttering, loping merrily with their handlers across the ring. I really wanted a horse. In truth, I wanted to *be* a horse, but Afghan hounds hit my preteen G-spot. Those runway-model-type show dogs seem absurd to me now— cartoonish, a crush left behind. These days, it's greyhounds.

People have been walking them around our neighborhood for years. They're like the ballet students I used to see near Lincoln Center on the way from my apartment in Hell's Kitchen to my starving-actor/ waitress gig on Columbus Avenue—long-legged Balanchine hopefuls in flocks of three or four. Hair in sleek little buns; elegant posture, slim as reeds; almost identical but not quite. Blue-jeaned Degas swans idling serenely, languidly, past lead-footed duck mortals.

Consulting with Eliza about dog options felt like punching an unhealed bruise—a sad reminder that she's only home for a min- ute, going back to college in Virginia after Christmas, having just finished a junior fall abroad in Tuscany. Ben and Sam are in their last year of high school, though, and it seems only right to have them weigh in before committing.

I don't enjoy the idea of my children feeling like houseguests with no say in what goes on. Just like three years ago, when Eliza was finishing high school, everything is so charged and bitter-sweet with the boys this fall—their last homecoming weekend, last Halloween. We're drowning in college applications. Because they're twins, the whole process has been complicated. Eliza's summer of touring colleges back in 2006 made for good practice—it was a high priority for her that college be only a short day's drive from home, so visiting was fairly civilized. These boys are looking all over the place. Sam and I executed a massive assault of the West Coast last summer—he says he thinks the warmer climate will be good for his sinuses. (Subtext: *You are too obsessed with my well-being. I need to get as far away from you as possible.*)

Ben is applying to schools in Michigan and Texas that he hasn't even had a chance to look at yet. At least the boys actually do overlap on New England schools. David was able to help with New England, even though travel is a challenge for him. He has tons of allergies to all kinds of things—chiefly foods, air fresheners, and the artificial smoke they use on movie sets. Organizing a trip that won't make David sick can be a very big operation. Given that he has to travel so much for work, I'd tried to limit his participation in the great college tour.

Everyone always asks if the twins will go away to school together. Apparently not. I get the impression they're determined to forge their own paths, and the prospect of losing my grip on everyone is disturbing. There will be no rest for me when the flock is scattered.

When they were all little and kidnappable, Sam used to have a way of disappearing at the mall or an amusement park. I was fanatically strict about keeping the children close, which they each processed in personal ways. Eliza would cling to my side like an octopus, positive that at any second someone would leap at us and tear her away from me. This made it hard to walk in a straight line. Ben (who had been the first twin to pop out of the womb) wanted, appropriately, to go everywhere first. But he understood he mustn't wander too far ahead, so he'd walk *right* in front of me, almost touching. I would have to keep asking Ben to step up the pace so Eliza and I wouldn't trip on his heels.

Sam didn't really seem to want to be associated with us, but he knew if he strayed too far I'd haul him back and make a mortifying public spectacle, forcing him to hold my hand. So he would usually loiter a little behind our clump and to one side, which was a blind spot in my peripheral vision. The kids still imitate me spinning around in urgent terror: *Where's SAM?* This would happen every ten minutes or so whenever we went out in crowds. *OH MY GOD—WHERE'S SAM?*

I should count my blessings. At least my children are not going to war. I have a couple of friends who have dealt with this, and it blows my mind. Pamela, who's a little older than I am, managed a relatively steady acting career while raising her son, Trevor, solo in L.A. Pamela is tough as nails. She had to be. After his senior year in high school, Trevor decided the best way to achieve higher education, given their financial situation, would be to join the Army. This was in 1990. The Gulf War started right after Trevor enlisted, and off he went to Desert Storm. I don't know how Pamela survived, let alone Trevor. I'd have been falling asleep in front of the news every night, waking alone in the wee hours with a lurch: *OH MY GOD—WHERE'S TREVOR?*

Full disclosure: I feel nothing but awe, gratitude, and respect for the military. My father served proudly in World War II. But I have read John Irving's *A Prayer for Owen Meany* more times than I can keep track of. Meaning, it's a good thing my boys were only nine years old on 9/11, because if Ben or Sam had expressed any inclination to sign up that year, I would have seriously considered sneaking into their bedrooms with my garden shears at night to lop off the tips of their trigger fingers.

My older sister, Colette, tries to help me keep things in perspective; she's this odd schizoid hybrid of Pollyanna and Chicken Little. *(Look, Sizzle, the sky is falling! Isn't it GORGEOUS?!)* Colette has lived across the pond for years with her husband, Badger, deep in the British countryside, and she's an avid news hound, always alert to what horrific disasters might befall the Morse family at any given moment, and always generous enough to take the trouble to tell me. She got me a little worked up last summer, just before Eliza left for Tuscany:

    —*Colette, it's Tuscany. What could possibly happen in Tuscany?*

    —*Um. You've heard about the earthquake, right?*

    —*Earthquake?*

    —*I'm sure she'll be fine because she's had so much experience, but remind her there was a 6.3 magnitude quake in central Italy last spring. The whole country is on a fault line.*

—Christ. That girl CANNOT go through a second earthquake.

—I wouldn't worry, Sizzle. It just happened, so there probably won't be another one for years. I'm so excited for Eliza! And you do know there have been four deaths from swine flu in Italy so far, right? I'm sure you'll send her with emergency medicine just in case. And of course you'll tell her to watch out for the men.

—I know, I know, European men assume that American girls are loose. That's what they warned me about when I went to France in high school Aren't we more global now?

—Not in Italy. They're very chauvinistic, but they're clever enough to hide it until they've got you in their power. The men will be all over Eliza, and if she sleeps with one of them he'll think she's easy and turn on her. But if she doesn't sleep with them, they will try to marry her and get her pregnant, and then they won't let her work. It happens all the time. They don't believe in women working, and they are EXTREMELY seductive.

—MARRIED?! God.

—Does she know about Foxy Knoxy?

—What's Foxy Knoxy?

—Oh my, haven't you heard about Amanda Knox yet, Sizzle? It's all over the news here; maybe you'll be more aware of it in the States when the trial heats up. A lovely British girl named Meredith Kercher was murdered in an especially spooky weird way. Meredith's roommate was Amanda Knox, an American college student, just like Eliza. She was in Perugia on her semester abroad—isn't Perugia right near where Eliza is going?

—*I don't know. Wait, let me look it up. . . .*

—*So Amanda Knox's lovely British roommate was horribly murdered. It was possibly satanic, and the* polizia *think Amanda and her Italian boyfriend did it. They are in jail, on trial for murder. This could happen, Sizzle. You have to prepare Eliza.*

—*Oh my gosh! Perugia's only thirty miles from where Eliza will be!*

—*Sizzle, don't worry. But tell her to avoid the non-Italian men too. There's been a lot of international sex-slave trafficking.*

—*Stop it. You're scaring me. Can I send her over to you on Easy Jet if anything bad starts to happen?*

—*Of course! We'd love it, but make sure she knows that Easy Jet cancels flights all the time. We are simply dying to have her, Sizzle; this is going to be so much fun!!!*

—*So much fun. My only daughter is going off for an idyllic semester in the Italian countryside, where she will either contract deadly swine flu, be murdered by Satanists, or become a barefoot pregnant married sex slave in jail. If she tries to escape, she will be swindled at the airport by some dodgy British puddle-jumper outfit. And then, while she's wandering penniless over the unforgiving Tuscan wasteland, an obscure, previously dormant fault line in the earth will open under her feet and swallow her up. Can't wait.*

Colette calls me Sizzle. She and Badger are semiretired, partly due to health, and they have no children, partly due to same. Instead, they have another kind of dog I'm drawn to: a lurcher. There are all different kinds of lurchers, each the direct product of a cross between a sight hound (meaning a greyhound, borzoi, Irish wolfhound, and the like—a hunting dog designed for speed and exceptional sight) and any other breed. Lurchers have the physique I covet, even though they're still basically mutts. Centuries ago, the English Forest Laws banned commoners from hunting with greyhounds, and I gather poachers used to sneak their ordinary Heinz 57–type female hunting dogs into the nobles' kennels under cover of darkness to breed with the nobles' fancy greyhounds. Lurchers are still used for all sorts of illegal sporting activities today, and the injured ones are often "retired" by the side of the road. England has an extensive lurcher rescue network.

Colette's lurcher, Spider, is the perfect combination of lord and scalawag—he has the characteristic narrow head and long, graceful limbs I'm so taken with, all covered with the most adorable topcoat of wiry gray tendrils. By rights, this dog should be mine. On visits to England I spend most of my time prowling after Spider with my camera, like a lovesick paparazzo.

Spider

I've heard of people spending large sums of money importing lurchers to the States, but I can't justify doing that with so many local dogs needing homes. The solution for us is obvious: a greyhound.

—*Lovely idea, Sizzle. I'm sure you'll be consulting all your local experts.*

—*Experts? It's not like we've never had a dog, Coco.*

—*You're right. It's so rewarding to teach yourself as you go. That's what I did at first, and I learned so much, especially after our first lurcher almost died when he spotted a deer on a walk, slipped his leash, and completely shredded all the skin up and down his legs dashing across a recently mown cornfield. Till then, I couldn't possibly have put together that sight hounds will never come reliably when called and have unusually fragile skin and all sorts of other unexpected vulnerabilities. You're so smart, Sizzle, of course you'll figure out how to manage an adult, undomesticated rescue dog that's had years to develop a grab bag of unpredictable emotional issues that might be impossible to fix.*

I absolutely adore my sister. Sometimes she's a little bit of a buzzkill.

We went to meet a couple of these otherworldly creatures at our neighbors', and, to my relief, even David was sold. The O'Brien dogs, Dylan and King, are not all waggly and knock-around like a Lab or a shepherd. They're incredibly sweet, and they like to have fun, just in their own particular fashion. Greyhounds are different in all kinds of unexpected ways. One thing I didn't realize is that they do not actually sit much—it's something about the way their frames are built. Linda O'Brien says they can sort of sit, but because their butts don't actually hit the floor, it's not really comfortable. This information has caused me some embarrassment. Our garden is riddled with proof of my ignorant yearning: sculptures of falsely posed greyhounds seated erect, like sentinels.

Linda's dogs prefer to rest on their massive chests (amazing sculpted affairs like the hull of a Viking ship), their fine, long front legs stretched out in front, ears pricked, everything symmetrical; the slimmest of sphinxes. Glamour and elegance aside, the wonder of Linda's dogs is that they are still dogs. King likes to bring out his toys to show visitors. Dylan is smart, a charming gentleman, always engaged with great interest in what's going on around him. Excellent hosts.

With David on board I'm now hell-bent. I *have* to have a greyhound of my very own, and I've been doing my best to prepare by reading up: *Retired Racing Greyhounds for Dummies*, of course, and *The Reign of the Greyhound*, by Cynthia A. Branigan, a veteran of the rescue movement. Branigan provides lots of colorful history: Greyhounds go back thousands of years—there are drawings of them in old Egyptian temples, and they're the only breed of dog mentioned in the bible. Alexander the Great named a city after a personal favorite, his courageous greyhound Peritas, said to have attacked the elephant of a Persian king during battle. Renaissance artists were as mad for these dogs as I—they're all over those wonderful tapestries of *The Hunt of the Unicorn*. Greyhounds went on the Crusades, somehow survived the Dark Ages, and traveled with Christopher Columbus on his second voyage to the New World. Gen. George Custer had a whole pack of greyhounds; he napped on the ground with them at camps between campaigns, and took them out coursing on the plains the day before the Battle of Little Big Horn. The more I read, the more determined I feel, fueled by a centuries-old fever for these iconic animals, so many of whom are now desperately in need of homes.

The rescue association really grills you; the application was like being handcuffed in a dark room with a harsh light shining in my eyes. They try to trip you up with all kinds of suspiciously loaded questions:

- *Why do you want a greyhound?* (Excuse me, but this is purely a humane and selfless gesture of fellowship to an animal in need. I utterly resent the implication my interest has anything to do with Empty Nest Syndrome, or creepy midlife crisis fetishism of any kind whatsoever.)

- *List all previous pets you have owned, how long you owned them, and the reason you no longer have them.* (Arrow *had* to be put down; she had a tumor, honest. Okay, okay, please don't hurt me; the tumor wasn't *actually* inoperable, but the vet said it was going to burst any second, causing her *horrible agony and certain death*, and Arrow was too old to take a chance on surgery, I swear!)

- *Where do your animals sleep?* (This is about the cats, right? Look, the cats kept waking the children up when they were little, so we made them sleep in the basement. Not the *children,* the *cats*; jeez! But that was in our old house, and they had *really comfy* beds. . . .)

- *You have children?* (I don't think these teenagers count as children; they're taller than *me*. They're almost gone anyway. I'd rather not talk about it.)

Greyhounds' reflexes are like lightning. They can never be let off the leash without a fence (meaning a physical fence—when a greyhound takes off, the electric jolt from an invisible barrier will kick in too late). And the biggest issue of all is Joey the cat, Arrow's black-and-white hunting partner. Greyhounds can go from zero to just over forty miles per hour in three strides. They are sprinters: bred, trained, and rewarded specifically for chasing little fluffy rabbitlike prototypes at top speed for about thirty seconds at a

time, with intent to kill. It's what they live for at the track, literally, and the rescue people have told me that because of Joey they'll
only give us a "cat tested" dog without a strong prey drive.

—Wait, you'll give us a dog? I passed the test? I can *have* one?
Oh my gosh, when? Oh thank you, thank you, okay I'll go straight
to Pet Value—what kind of food—oh and a coat. They need coats
in winter, right? I'll get a coat—

—No. Please don't buy anything till we're sure you'll make a
good match. We've just e-mailed you pictures of a three-year-old
female named Lilly—tell us what you think.

What I *think*? I'm having a fit. She's skinny as a rail, sweet
brown eyes, ears a little cockeyed—oh my gosh, how adorable—
and she's brindle! My favorite! Greyhounds come in all different
shades (the rarest is gray, oddly, which they refer to as "blue"), but
I didn't dare spoil my chances by specifying. Brindles are striped—
one of the O'Brien dogs, King, is a brindle, but King's a bit darker
than Lilly, who is fawn with black stripes, like a tiger—perfect!
In one picture she's chomping on some kind of stuffed animal,
looking happy, so of course I have to rush out to the store. My dog
needs toys!

4.

Lilly [*sic*]

DECEMBER 2009

That mean black-and-white rabbit is up in the tree again.

In Crate-land they wet us with a hose, not the sky. In this place there is no us. There's only you, and the wet here is an unknown outside thing that will hurt you. It freezes up your insides so you don't feel like doing it at all; you just can't, even though it's your first time out today and you have been walked (dragged) around several times until you are shivering like crazy.

She says, "Awww poor Lilly."

And then you can go back inside and shake it all off. She laughs, and dries you some more (her scent is perfect!). Then you can have your breakfast and wait in your crate and think about it.

You can still see her. Good. You keep a close eye while she talks to her box.

"Hi, Linda, it's Susan again, sorry. How about I dip her paws in hot water to make her do her business in the rain?"

She pulls out the brown thing with all the hooks and wraps it around you. It must be all right, because she is from heaven. She has treats. (And oh, the scent of her! You could die for her.)

She says, "Do you think you can do it with your coat on, Lilly?" *and she takes (drags) you out again.*

She says, "We won't go back in until you are not afraid of being out here."

And THEN she lets you off the leash in the big yard, and you decide to sniff all over it, as long as she is right next to you.

Big wind never happens in Crate-land. She says, "Crikey," *and you go hide with her under the mean black-and-white rabbit's tree. And because you are less cold with the brown hooks thing on, it begins to feel more like an adventure.*

She says, "Okay, Lilly, seriously."

You just ignore her, because what an idea, trying to squat when you're trapped in this crazy brown thing. And you walk around some more with her, and then she bends over (that scent!) and takes it off. And suddenly you feel like doing it, so you do both kinds.

She says, "Glad that's over for f^%#'s sake," *and finally you can go back inside.*

I'm not quite clear how this happened. I remember a minivan pulling up to the house, and I know a dog hopped out of the back. It came into the house with me, and I immediately presented it with a toy, which it accepted with great enthusiasm, and everyone cheered. The rest is a blur. I think I fell into some kind of enraptured trance, muttering under my breath, *Yes keep her yes yes yes.* The rescue people spent a long time inspecting the height of our fence, but they must not have been concerned by my condition, because now they're gone, and Lilly is not. She's landed, like a disoriented tiger-striped neutron bomb.

A waist-high crate is taking up half the dining room. Every floor has a huge dog bed now, because a greyhound's skin is too thin even for carpets. You have to put coats on them when the temperature dips below 40 degrees, and I bought all kinds: lightweight fleece for everyday, turtleneck for snow. My favorite is a brown barn-type quilted raincoat I found. It has hooks, like a horse blanket—and it goes perfectly with Lilly's new braided leather leash. The rescue lady was very stern and ceremonial about that leash. I had to promise to put the handle over my wrist and wrap the strap twice around my hand before she would let go.

Greyhounds use specially elevated food bowls—their giraffe necks might get a crick from bending all the way to the floor.

We're keeping the name the rescue people gave her when

she first left the track. It's likely the racetrack staff didn't teach this dog to respond to the sexless, impersonal professional name on Lilly's papers, CL Lighting. My feeling is she's had her share of upheaval. It's not like me to pass up an opportunity to be snotty about that double *l (What exactly did they have in mind, a flower or a preppy dress designer?)* but something tells me this dog has already been through enough change for a lifetime. She's Lilly, and that's that.

I think James Cameron's designer must have used a dog like Lilly as visual inspiration for the creatures in the movie *Avatar.* Her brindle stripes are a dead giveaway—black-on-fawn eyeliner fanning out Cleopatra-style from the outer corners of her eyes. Every rib shows—you can literally see daylight through skin stretched over the tendons on the backs of Lilly's hind legs. At night, picking her way around the yard, slipping in and out of shadows in the moonlight, she really does look like a mysterious creature from another world. She's missing part of one ear and most of the fur on her haunches, and she is going to take a while to settle in. I am beside myself with delight.

And boy is Joey pissed. Lilly's still on cat probation; wearing a muzzle when he's around. Joey spends most of his days glowering out at me from deep inside the mattress frame of a guest bed on our third floor.

It's Christmas vacation. Eliza's been home from her semester in Tuscany since Thanksgiving, and there's not a single scratch on her. David is happily between jobs. The boys are working systematically through masses of college applications. Joey's found a nice, safe tree in the yard, and Lilly—well. Lilly is trying. For some reason, she can't bear to let me out of her sight.

The rescue people told me I had to aggressively bond with her at first, and I think I may have overdone it. Lilly is even more infatuated with me than I am with her, if such a thing is possible. I'm extremely flattered—it's sort of like being befriended by the coolest kid in your fifth-grade class—but I'm also feeling a little like a hostage. I can't leave her much, because if David or the boys are in charge, Lilly barks incessantly no matter how nice they are to her. (*Mama, she won't shut up. She thinks we're going to kill her.*) She definitely senses the difference between men and women—she will tolerate Eliza, but if one of our men so much as looks at her she will literally get up and run out of the room. David says Lilly actually cringes when he reaches to pet her.

For a greyhound rescued off the track, everything is a first, and it's overwhelming. Lilly has no reference point for the simplest things. She's not dimwitted; quite the opposite—the rescue people gave me her racing records and Linda O'Brien is impressed. Dylan and King were retired from racing almost immediately, whereas Lilly actually won a few races over the years.

I'm sensing Lilly's career success is part of her problem. She's three years old and now she has to learn a whole new way of life. She's been handled a lot by humans, but not in a domestic situation. They say her trainer was one of the good ones, but still, there are these haunting scars—the slightly shredded ear, and a bald patch on her shoulder that looks like the result of a particularly nasty accident. A total mystery. She's spent her entire life in a crate, only turned out a few times a day, and raced, raced, raced, always in the company of other greyhounds, so this new lifestyle must be overwhelming; even something as inoffensive as the *Brrring* of a doorbell can throw her in a tailspin. And when these dogs are stressed, they go rigid; they're incredibly strong. When they freeze in place, the greyhound people call it "statue-ing up," and that's exactly right. It's like trying to coax an iron statue that's psychically bolted itself to the floor.

Stairs were the worst. The rescue people recommend Lilly sleep in our bedroom, which is fine with us. But at first, maneuvering this creature up to our second floor was ridiculously hard. There are no stairs at the track, and greyhound bodies are not built for them anyway. You can't blame them; it's a matter of engineering. I heard about this one lady who couldn't lure her new greyhound up stairs for anything. If she tried to sleep in her bedroom, the dog would cry all night, so she slept downstairs on their sofa for months. She finally caved and adopted a second greyhound to keep the first one company at night.

I can't get a second dog. David is thinking about doing a television series once the boys go to college. A television series would take months out of every year with a six-year commitment, and I have promised I'll go on location with him. I might be able to figure out a way to bring one dog, but two? And besides, a second greyhound could come with a whole new set of problems, making everything even more complicated. I've heard of this happening from other adopters. Forget it. This lovely animal deserves a good retirement, but there are limits. We'll figure it out.

She says, "Here we go Lilly, it's bedtime," *and she goes up that thing that wants to break your legs, leaving you down here with THEM, and they are all standing waaay too close.*

They're saying, "Go on, Lilly," *and you just ignore them, so she starts to come back.*

But the one, the one with the hairy face, says, "Stay up there, Susan, she'll follow you."

She says, "She will NOT, David. Lilly never does. I have to put her feet on the stairs one at a time all the way to the top like they showed me."

And oh, you will not, you will not.

She takes your front paws and forces them up there. She gets behind you and says, "Aargh, my back," *and shoves your haunches up so you have to move your front paws ahead.*

She says, "That's right, keep going, oooh I stubbed my toe, dammit," *and gives you another shove and Whoops, you're climbing, and it's too slippery and your toenails can't find anything.*

She says, "Man, her legs are so skinny, I'm scared she'll fall backwards and break something but she's so frigging strong!"

"Keep going, Lilly, YES!!! Good girl!!" *All of them are cheering— horrible.*

She yells, "Sam and Ben, I can't come back down there now

or she'll follow me. I'm counting on you to finish your college supplement essays."

And then you go in this quiet place and here's your bed. Phew.

Someone remind me why this was a good idea.

E.T. has arrived from his planet and moved in with us, like a gift. But our E.T. is strong as an ox, she weighs almost seventy pounds, and she is completely fixated on me.

5.

Nothing Is Broken

What is it about the twins' impending departure that feels so particularly stressful? Is it because they seem to have such devastating confidence about leaving home, or is it because they're our last? The final two dazed rabbits pulled out of a magician's hat at the end of a show, shooed offstage to face Lord knows what kind of rabbitish perils?

It definitely helps having Lilly for company. She's still deeply reserved, which fascinates me—clearly she wants to see where I am at all times, but actual interaction is not really a priority—an odd combination of need and detachment. I think her clinging has to do with being afraid this new, quiet, comfortable life with carpets and beds is all about me, and if I disappear she might have to go back to the concrete work camp. She sort of handles me the same strategic way I do the boys these days, come to think of it; determined to keep tabs without interfering too much. Every day there's some new obstacle for her to decipher. Snow has been a major challenge, which makes perfect sense on reflection—Lilly has never lived anywhere but Florida and Texas. We're having an extreme winter this year, and it's been tedious figuring out how to convince her to even step in snow when she's not forced by a leash, let alone relieve herself, given she has to be bundled up Charlie Brown–style, to protect her thin skin. *(You know she is waiting for you to do it, but where? The ground is gone!)* A work in progress.

David is doing his best to woo her. He reports that as long as he pays lots of attention to Lilly when I'm out, her panic eventually shifts and she sort of accepts him as a poor substitute, following him around the house the way she does me. But as soon as I'm home, she goes back to being utterly indifferent to him, if not actually hostile. We are trying to help Lilly associate David with pleasure, so whenever possible, he prepares her meals. She'll accept food from him with some reservations, but petting is not permitted, which is very sad for David. He's determined to win her over, though, and through trial and error, he's figured out one special trick. Lilly will leave the room if David approaches her from the front, no matter how unthreateningly. But if he turns around and backs up to her very, very slowly, one tiny step at a time, she doesn't retreat. And once he's backed up enough to be standing beside her, she'll actually let him touch her, which, she is learning, can be quite pleasant. David gives great backrubs.

One step in the right direction: Lilly doesn't need the muzzle anymore around Joey. During the prescribed three-week muzzled introductory period, Joey pretty much spent all his indoor time either locked in my office with his food dish and litter box, or tangled in those bedsprings up on the third floor. We'd occasionally drag him out, sit them down next to each other, and tell them both what great friends they were going to be. Neither seemed to buy it.

The muzzle business was weird for us, even though Lilly appeared to take it in stride. It helped to know that greyhounds always wear them when they race—they're pretty much an athletic accessory, like shin guards or a jock strap—but we did look forward to the night we could finally take that muzzle off. It was dinnertime. Joey, who has been a little peckish lately, was dining in my office as usual. Everyone else was gathered around the kitchen table, Lilly napping unmuzzled on her bed by my chair. At the end of the meal we decided it was now or never, and Ben was dispatched to release Joey from the office. We all held our breath, waiting to see what would happen.

Joey seemed to know something was up as soon as he reached the kitchen. In fact, it was as if he'd spent the whole muzzle period plotting exactly how to make the most of this first teachable moment. What he did was creepy, but in hindsight quite brilliant.

First, Joey paused briefly at the threshold to assess the situation (silent audience of humans at the table, unmuzzled killer dog asleep on the floor). He then pivoted smoothly off to the right, walking most of the kitchen's perimeter so as to approach his target from behind.

I've been around plenty of heated first encounters between dogs and cats. I thought I knew what to expect, but I've never seen a cat do anything like what Joey did to Lilly that night. He'd clearly figured out he was dealing with more than your average housedog. He was practically rehearsed, and utterly confident. Joey didn't growl, spit, or puff up his tail; no blood was drawn—he never had to unsheathe a single claw. Instead, he marched right up to Lilly from behind, and—*Squish!* Joey rammed his little nose directly into Lilly's butthole as far as possible.

Greyhounds' tails are very skinny. There's hardly any fur back there, so their buttholes are easy to locate. This was not your average animal-handshake-type thing; there was nothing even remotely sociable going on. Joey performed with surgical precision, as if he really *meant* it, in a creepy S&M prison-rape sort of way, causing Lilly to bolt awake with a yelp and shoot out of the room. *(There is something* wrong *with that rabbit!)*

That was that. Joey sat down and started cleaning himself: *You are now my bitch, dog.*

Voice mail from Mother Brigid:

Ech-ehhmmm. It's Ma. Susie? I can't hear you. What's wrong with this thing? Ech-ech-ehhmmm. Are you there, Susie? I think my phone may be broken. Put this by the bed, Doris, or Florence. Oh. Florida. Sorry. Thank you, Florida. I'm calling my daughter back now.

(Scuffling noises followed by *BOOP BERP BEEP BOP BOOP*: the jarring, distinctly recognizable melody of my touchtone number—she has forgotten to disconnect before redialing.)

(Silence.)

Susie? Oh dear. . . .

Now, Dor . . . erm . . . Florida, could you please bring me the honey from the little cupboard over the sink. The one that says "Local Honey"—tea with local honey is better for allergies because local bees pollinate local flowers, and that's what I'm allergic to. Ehhmm. I can't stop clearing my throat; it's dreadful.

Susie, are you there or not? Well. If this is me leaving you a message, then I have to tell you thank you very much for inviting me for New Year's

Eve but I promised Babbie I'd meet her at a party here this afternoon and I don't know how long it will go, so I think I'll be tired tonight.

(Extended silence.)

Thank you, Florence, this tea is perfect.

(Slurping noise.)

Ech-ehhmmm.

(More scuffling.)

Oh, and Susie, did you get an e-mail Father Nectarius sent for you to give me that has all the homilies by Saint Theophan the Recluse, and if you did, can you please bring it as soon as possible? It's urgent. And it's Ma. How is Lilly? God bless and call me back.

(Click.)

My mother has always taken up a huge chunk of my attention, partly because she won't have it any other way, and partly because I am a little fixated. She's extremely interesting, which is an understatement. My father used to say he hoped to die before Ma because his life would be too boring without her. I often wonder what he'd make of the new identity she's assumed since he left us fifteen years back.

Ma's kind of picky about her religions. After trying six or seven she settled, quite late in life, on Orthodox Christianity. I was skeptical about her level of commitment, but it seems this latest religion has stuck—as demonstrated a couple of years ago when an Orthodox bishop came along and made her a nun at age eighty-five on the eve of cancer surgery, and she almost took up permanent residence in a skilled nursing facility located inconveniently two hours from here in the farmlands of Carlisle, Pennsylvania, because it was close to her church.

But then, a luxury retirement community nearer to me offered a clergy scholarship of sorts. Confronted with a choice between frequent communion with the priests upstate, and the chance to spiritually enrich the life of her infidel youngest daughter (me) during her twilight years, Ma picked the latter. The priests in Carlisle gave their blessing on the condition that Mother Brigid (that's her nun name) stay in close touch, meaning visits on the high holy days, health permitting.

The distance has been a challenge. There are other clergy at the new place, but Ma's the only Orthodox. She follows the discipline as well as can be expected, given her infirm condition and particular upper-crusty sensibilities. Her financial-assistance package is fair but does not cover all the helpers we believe are required to keep Ma mellow—kind companions like Florida making tea—that's up to my siblings and me. It's truly lucky we can afford to help, because my mother is not the sort to suffer hardship easily, despite her monastic inclination.

As a nun, Mother Brigid wears no jewelry save a cross. All her clothes are black. *(Silk, linen, or cashmere. Nothing synthetic, if you please.)* There's nobody nearby to consult about things like what to do with the hair. Orthodox nuns and priests are not supposed to ever, ever cut their hair, and it's a challenge figuring out how to safely stow Ma's long white mane now that it's grown past her waist. I'm a bit worried the mane will come loose someday and get caught in the motor of the electric scooter she uses to jet around campus on her various social assignations.

Mother Brigid says her prayers daily; the priests check in whenever they can. The issue of e-mails keeps cropping up. The nearest Orthodox Christian clergy in our state are all in Carlisle. The rest are scattered throughout the United States and Canada, and they constantly send each other vital communications by e-mail—e-mails Mother Brigid misses out on because she doesn't have a computer. If I print and hand-deliver all the stuff they send me for her I'll wipe out half the forests on the planet, for Lord's sake.

A computer is out of the question. Ma has been techno-impaired for as long as I can remember; it's not an age thing—she can barely operate her cordless phone. I tried giving her a castoff iMac and an e-mail address some years ago, just as an experiment, back in the pre–Mother Brigid era when logging into e-mail was a long and complicated process better left to younger generations. Ma was extremely motivated to learn, but all our emergency problem-solving phone sessions were totally unproductive, like an endless bumper-car ride to nowhere:

　　—This computer is definitely broken.

　　—Nothing is broken, Ma. You turned it on, right?

　　—Oh. How do I do that?

　　—See the button on the bottom of the screen?

　　—Wait a minute. I'm in the bedroom.

　　(Clump clump clump.)

　　—All right, what am I looking for?

—*There's a round button down on the right. Push it.*

(A loud blaring noise erupts in the background.)

—*Susie, what on earth is that racket?*

—*I don't know. Did the screen turn on? What do you see?*

—*What? It's too noisy in here.*

—*MA. WHAT DO YOU SEE ON THE SCREEN?*

—*I see Fox. Oh, I can't bear it.*

—*You see a fox? What's wrong with it? Never mind. Are there any words on the screen?*

—*There's a new pope. He's waving from the balcony of the Vatican.*

—*Ma.*

—*Honestly, the Catholics. Look at them all adoring him and rejoicing.*

—*MA. That's Fox News on the television.*

—*What?*

—*TURN THE TELEVISION OFF, MA. GO OVER TO YOUR DESK AND TURN ON THE THING THAT SAYS IMAC.*

I can't rush over to Ma's with these e-mailed Recluse homilies. I don't even have time to read my own e-mails right now. We're in the final stretch of the boys' college application process, and it's hell on so many levels.

Someone suggested to me once that the reason parents and teenagers clash has something to do with biological programming. Tempers are designed to flare because adolescents are supposed to go out into the world eventually, be fruitful, and multiply. If home is a totally happy, welcoming place for them, what's to leave?

It's not that bad; I do love our boys. Eliza's college application process three years ago was equally fraught, and after all that intensity her departure was a real shock to me—like being dumped by a first love. At Eliza's new campus they really knew how to milk the fall drop-off for parents of freshmen. We had two full days of family orientation events, climaxing with a huge rally in the sports arena. Parents sat in bleachers with their kids and listened to administrators crowing about all the exciting opportunities for this year's brilliant crop of scholars. Just when they had us convinced we were the luckiest families in the United States, they called the freshmen down to meet their perky orientation advisors, who would keep them busy for the rest of the evening, later herding them off to their first night in the dorms.

—Good-bye, parents, the dean trilled, as a thousand precious packages descended (raced) en masse down the aisles onto the floor of the stadium. Your chickens are safe! It's like stepping off a cliff. Nothing left to do but straggle out the arena's swinging glass doors and drive back to comfortless hotel rooms. Dumped. Counting the minutes till they doled out one final crumb: a parking-lot good-bye the next morning, out behind the dorms by the trash bins.

Mornings at home have been lonely since she left. David's a late sleeper, and, unlike the boys, Eliza believes in starting the day with a good meal. Breakfast was always our special mother-daughter time. Often we were so absorbed in yakking about this, that, and the other, I'd make her a little late for school. I had no idea how much this meant to me till that first fall without her. I'd set the alarm early as usual to make breakfast for the boys, knowing they'd never eat it and the only discourse I could expect would be a couple of grunts when they came galumphing down the stairs and careened out the door.

While I waited for the privilege of serving cinnamon toast (more likely slinging it at the back of Sam and Ben's car as it shot down the driveway), I'd light the kettle, pull a dirty "College Mom" mug I'd received at Eliza's orientation out of the cluttered dishwasher, and rinse it by hand. No other vessel would do those first raw mornings, scraping butter on toast, weeping into my English Breakfast, debating whether or not to pick up the phone if it rang, knowing the odds were it would NOT be Eliza calling but my mother, probably asking how to turn off her radio. *(Susie, I want to get it to STOP. I don't want this thing on; it's perfectly awful. It's some NPR program and it's just dreadful about bisexual HIPPOS or something. Baboons. And the woman said one of them grabbed her. Disgusting.)*

At least Lilly really needs me, even if her constant shadowing has been a bit tiresome. More and more, I'm coming to understand the use of pets as a subconscious substitute for children. I'll never forget seeing a photo of my friend Francesca holding their new puppy, Emma. Francesca and her husband were discussing the possibility of a third child at the time—she had a strong maternal urge that wasn't satisfied yet, and her husband wasn't completely ready. So they got

Emma, sort of to tide Francesca over, I'm guessing. This photo of Francesca holding Emma in her arms, practically in breastfeeding position, keeps popping into my head these days. Is Lilly's attention something I encourage subliminally because I fear losing the children? I think I'm going to have to forget I asked that question.

I feel a little bad for Joey. He's definitely out of sorts. I wonder if he's off his feed because Lilly's arrival has stirred up his grief at losing Arrow? I can certainly relate—the boys' preparations do make me think of Eliza. A friend, Tandy, says she'll never forget running into me in the parking lot of the Super Fresh a few days after Eliza's freshman drop-off.

—*How are you?* Tandy asked, expecting the standard *Fine, how are you?*

Instead, I fell into Tandy's arms, pointing to something I'd just spotted on my shopping list—an obsolete entry in Eliza's loopy script.

—*She wanted Nutri-Grain bars!!!*

Eliza's a college junior now. I've had three years to absorb and trust what Tandy assured me of that day: *They're not really gone. They come back.*

David seems to understand this concept instinctively—all the time he's spent on location, he's become an old hand at good-byes. He processed Eliza's departure philosophically, especially compared to me, and, as it turned out, Tandy was right. Eliza does come home, like clockwork. It is true: You're thrilled they're home. Over the moon with delight, really. But you're kind of used to the reduction in your chore load, and you sort of wish they'd not expect you to do anything extra for them anymore. *(If she really wants Nutri-Grain bars that badly, why can't she go to the market and pick up a box?)*

Because David is away so much, the process of applying for college and other academic minutiae is mostly my job. With my stay-at-home status, it is logical that I'm the one our offspring will turn to when it comes time to hit that final Submit button on the Common Application website. David is on call if we need him, but for the most part it's easier to leave him on the sidelines, in the kitchen making dinner if possible. (I hate cooking, and David's an absolute master. He has tons of food allergies, so he puts a lot of thought into inventing fantastic new recipes. He is an artist. Each meal is a symphony.)

Ben seems to be squared away. He and his girlfriend, Jilli, have been sitting side by side on the sofa for weeks, meticulously perfecting their applications, keeping each other on course. Jilli's mother is a college guidance counselor, so I am under the impression we can actually take the old-fashioned approach with Ben's admission process, sort of like back when I was applying myself. Parents were allowed to stay out of it then, and everything somehow fell into place. Quite relaxing compared to Eliza's frantic process, and this cauldron of stress with Sam. It's lucky Mother Brigid has that party this afternoon and is staying out of my hair, because I'm kind of climbing the walls.

It's New Year's Eve morning and Sam is on the last lap. He's been hard at it all week, now facing tonight's midnight deadline for his big Ivy League reach. These Ivies are a real shot in the dark for most high school seniors given the competitive climate baby boomers' kids face these days, and quite frankly, we admire the kid's guts going for the gold.

Sam chose this Ivy because a lot of his forebears were happy there, and also because it is distinguished as being particularly artsy and humanities-focused, which is a good fit for him. He has finally finished polishing his short answers—a series of quick questions like *Why did you choose to apply to Ivy University?* and so forth—now he's tackling the big essay.

While Sam works, I burn off some of my nervous energy on a rather long and invigorating walk with Lilly. Thankfully there's no snow on the ground at the moment. These walks are a lot more fun than they were when she first arrived. When everything was new, she was on sensory overload and it was all I could do to drag her up the block and back. For a while, the only way to mobilize her was to coordinate our walk schedule with the O'Briens' and travel in a pack, like racetrack dogs. Now Lilly loves a walk. She's becoming more and more interested in her surroundings, slowing down when we pass people on the sidewalk, disappointed if we don't stop to say hello. Usually we do—most people are struck by her regal bearing, her glamorous markings. Walking with Lilly is a little like being out with David when people want to talk movies or take a picture.

Today, we ramble all over the neighborhood and there are lots of squirrels for Lilly to go all instantly rigid and muscular about, ears pricked forward like tiger-striped torpedoes. It's awfully primal when she spots small rabbitlike prey. Unlike Arrow, who used to yank me everywhere, Lilly has wonderful walking manners as long as her prey drive isn't triggered. Her leash stays deceptively slack until she sights something, so it's important to always be ready, because her contained energy sort of shoots electrically up the leash and you are suddenly very aware you're walking a canine superhero.

I don't have the mental capacity to think of anything more creative than cheese and crackers for lunch. While I'm munching I check our voice mail again:

Susie, have they called you yet? I hope you're not worried, because it's all right, really. I mean, it was frightening, but no harm done because that woman I backed into with the scooter at the party today is fine, thank heavens, although it was a little touch and go at first when she fell down and we were very upset until she was able to get up from the floor. So please don't worry and I hope everything's fine with the boys.

And God bless. Call me back. It's Ma, and I'm so much better now I really don't think I need the scooter anymore anyway. It was very useful for a while, but I think for now they'd better keep it.

Because the party was too crowded, you know, and I couldn't see where I was going at all. And I'm very glad that woman's leg braces weren't damaged in the slightest. So call me back.

SUSAN MORSE

I call. The scooter has been confiscated, and Ma's supposed to take a month to think about what she's done. Then, maybe, she can have her vehicle back, like a senior-citizen time-out. Tomorrow, when the Ivy U application is finally over with, I'll have to go see her. Visits have been interesting lately. I bring Lilly whenever possible, but she's extremely nervous in the car. I don't think she has ever traveled in a regular passenger vehicle. She won't lie down on the backseat, and because of her long flamingo legs I've been quite worried she'd fall into the seat well and break something. Even her tail can be an issue. I can't get over all the many ways greyhounds can injure themselves—you wouldn't think a dog's tail would be all that vulnerable, but I've heard stories about greys who get so excited when the leash comes out, they whack their tails against something and actually break the skin. They don't feel it, though, and they keep on wagging, and then there's this sort of loose garden hose, geysering blood all over the walls like a doggie horror movie.

My car's backseat now has an elaborate strapped-in dog cover that at least provides Lilly a flat surface. She can stand safely behind me, her needle nose thrust in agitation as far as possible between my headrest and the window, seeking comfort. I try to remember to bring treats, because once we arrive, Ma is mostly disapproving if Lilly is too stressed to relate to her.

—*Susie, this dog won't do. It's much too damaged.*

—*She just needs time, Ma.*

Nothing is broken.

I have a feeling my cheese-and-cracker lunch was not such a good idea—too much dairy. We are having our traditional New Year's Eve fondue tonight (just us, the kids, and David's mother), followed by a movie. Usually fondue prep is my job because David's allergic to everything in it. (Okay, that's a slight exaggeration. He can eat cheese. He just can't have the white wine, garlic, cornstarch, lemon juice, kirsch, or nutmeg. Basically anything that makes it taste good. Oh, and no bread. And I'm pretty sure his cheese has to be imported.) So on fondue nights while we crowd around the pot with our little spears to harpoon crusty chunks of French baguette and groan orgasmically about the *faaabulous* flavor of *Gruyèrrrre*, David sits watching, patient and uncomplaining, with his plate of rice pasta and broccoli.

I'd like to spare David the nonsense fondue requires (digging out the special forks, setting up the pot and the sterno, slicing all

that yummy bread), given he won't have the satisfaction of actually enjoying it once it's served tonight. But this year time is of the
essence; the boys have looming deadlines and I need to be available
right up till we hit that last Submit button with the final application
fee payment. Midnight's a ways off. I'm not stressing too much;
not yet, even though Sam is still trying to decide what his long Ivy
U essay will be about. He's kicking around an idea for one about
going to Toys"R"Us with Ben to choose a treat.

I used to dangle visits to Toys"R"Us as a reward for the kids
when they'd endured something particularly stressful, like being
vaccinated or having a tooth filled. We'd go straight to Toys"R"Us
from the doctor or dentist and let everyone pick out what they
wanted in a specific price range.

Eliza gravitated toward reliable standards like the Littlest Pet
Shop or My Little Pony. The boys' tastes were trickier.

Being the same sex and age it was natural for them to want the
same thing. Usually that thing had to involve batteries or chargers
or mechanisms of some kind, which meant it was safe to assume
the bloody device was bound to break. I would try to herd the boys
to an aisle with something straightforward, like maybe a ball or a
plastic dinosaur, but no. They had to have the bells and whistles—
swords that light up and make *Star Wars*–type noises were of particular interest. Those things should be banned.

What Sam found interesting fodder for his essay is that
after I paid for their identical and fabulous Super Sonic Death
Ray Whatsits (always checking carefully that the lights and the

Bzzzzzzz sound effect worked properly on both Whatsits by pushing the Test buttons in the store), we'd drive home as quickly as possible. By the time we reached our driveway, ripped packaging littering the floor of the car, Sam's Death Ray Whatsit would be stone-cold dead.

Not Ben's Whatsit. Ben's Whatsit worked great. It was Sam's. *Always* Sam's. As if he occupied some kind of magnetic field—you know those people whose wristwatches stop immediately when they put them on? I don't believe in curses, but Sam could make a case for it.

Ben and his Whatsit could joyfully dart all over the house for weeks: *Bzzzzzz! Bzzzzzzzzzzzzzzzz!* And there'd be Sam, in a corner, slumped mournfully over his identical but hatefully impotent Sonic Death Ray.

Broken.

And now Sam's trying to figure out what this tendency to pick the defective toy might signify in the grand scheme, moving forward into life as a master of the universe at Ivy U.

The fondue is superb. My secret is to make twice as much as the suggested portions, so we can all (except David) completely stuff ourselves. Sam says he's abandoned his broken-toy essay idea. He is going to write what he calls *My Philosophy*—a provocative treatise exploring the way his friends and the talking heads on television seemed unnecessarily narrow-minded in their opinions during the presidential election. He thinks people his age are much too young to be fixed in their beliefs and need to stay open to new ideas. *Not bad*, we tell him.

Eliza and Ben depart early to ring in the New Year with their friends. Must be nice; Sam is resigned to missing most of tonight's fun with his buddies, but he's hoping he can get out of here by midnight so he can drive to a friend's for a sleepover. David and his mother retire to watch a movie. I do dishes (*why* does cheese always stick to pots like frigging epoxy?) then pace in the next room.

Lilly follows, alert to my growing anxiety, her toenails keeping time. *Click-clack click-clack.*

Sam sits at the island in the kitchen with his laptop. *Tick-tock tick-tock.*

Wait a second. There is no sound of typing coming from that kitchen. The boy has gone into a torpor again, I know it.

Click-clack click-clack.

Tick-tock tick-tock.

Three hours to go.

What am I doing anyway? Nobody stood over me when I applied for college. I filled in my one application by hand, in *pen*, and stuck the thing in the mail with a check, and a month or so later I was accepted. End of story. What a world we live in now.

That boy needs a jump-start. Maybe I should go in there, grab one of the fondue forks off the dish drainer, and stab him with it.

At 11:38 p.m. Sam finally completes his long essay. All I do is skim it; at this point he could have written *I Think I Am A Child-Molesting Cannibal Terrorist From Outer Space* and I would have sent the piece in unchallenged because at least it's an essay. Maybe the admissions staff will be so swamped and buried under all the other essays about *What I Learned From My Dog When It Died* and *How Football Makes Me A Compassionate Citizen*, they won't have time to process Sam's anyway.

So Sam and I charge off with Lilly at our heels *(Hey! Where's she going? This is not okay; she has to wait for you—ouch, your toenails!)* to submit his long essay and all the other Ivy U short answers and whatnot on the newest computer in the house. We are positive the Common App site will be jammed this close to the midnight deadline with millions of dead dogs and compassionate football crap and we're going to need the best technology we've got.

When Sam tries to upload his first short answer, the supplement site rejects it three times. He's getting a little uptight and so am I. We have been here before, sitting in front of the Common App website applying to all Sam's other schools, grabbing the mouse from each other, elbowing, hissing, *No no Sam why did you click that you have to click that other thing, I did this with Eliza you have to let me do it.* And *Oh my God, Mama, stop it just calm down what is your problem.*

—It's BROKEN, Sam.

—No, it's not, Mama.

Nothing is broken.

Lilly is curled under the desk at my feet, even though the floor is very, very hard under there. She seems to feel this is the best place to be right now.

Sam, Lilly, and I log out and log back in to see if that helps. The first short answer about *Why I chose Ivy U* seems to be uploading; there's a sort of spinny thing next to it going round and round and round. *Tick-tock tick-tock.*

It is 11:41 p.m. Once this thing finishes spinning we still have to upload a few more short answers and the big long essay before we can finally hit Submit. Then Sam will have joined throngs of ancestors, at least as an applicant, at Ivy U.

Click. Rejected?!

—S%#F@^*# Sam, I'm right. Your Common Application is *broken*.

Our boys entered the world by vaginal delivery, which seems to impress people. Twins are often C-sectioned out, but we had a naturally oriented, hot-dog Southern California OBGYN with twin girls of his own who was confident he could make my dream of old-fashioned childbirth a reality.

I was justifiably nervous but determined to try. I did my homework during pregnancy, reading everything I could find about what to expect at delivery. One thing I found encouraging was that the first twin to arrive sort of opens the birth canal, making the second twin's entrance less excruciating for the mother. So you're literally getting two for the price of one, pain-wise.

Thing is, we weren't yet acquainted with Sam and his predisposition for last-minute drama and general Sonic Whatsit–type bad luck.

—Sam, you've been working all week and your friends are waiting. Your actual writing's all done, and I can't stand that this stupid clunky website is keeping you here on your last New Year's Eve of high school. Why don't you go? I'll just hand-type your short answers into the boxes if I have to. I swear on a stack of bibles I won't change anything.

In the middle of copying out *I am interested in Ivy U because everyone always tells me this is the best school for me* or something, I begin to get a major stomachache. The doubled-over childbirth kind. I am literally on the floor trying to reach up to the keyboard from under the desk, just to tap one more key, sweating; it's so awful. What's wrong with me? Oh, the fondue on top of the cheese at lunch.

What if I have to go to the emergency room and this thing never gets submitted oh no. . . .

Twelve minutes to midnight——crap! I crawl to the intercom and summon David to come help me, which is highly unusual. He has never laid eyes on a Common Application in his life and really has no idea what is going on. I just need him to check my typing to see if I have made any mistakes or changed Sam's writing in any way.

—He's used "really" twice in one paragraph.

—That's okay, David.

—Are you sure?

David hasn't had a chance to wrap his mind around all the nuances of college-application etiquette. He's right, of course, but Sam must express himself in his own way, leaving blemishes.

—David, the priority is authenticity.

I'm trying to explain this strategy from under the desk, next to Lilly, both of us curled up in balls together. *(She's so close!)* So it doesn't seem I'm being taken seriously, and, oh well, we ~~get rid of Sam's extra "really"~~ agree not to touch one hair on Sam's short essay's head. *Save.*

Now for the long essay. It's kind of comforting to birth this final application alone here, with my husband. Just the two of us.

And Lilly.

The twins were born sixteen minutes apart. With multiples, an interval longer than twenty minutes traditionally warrants an emergency C-section for the second birth, so we were cutting it close. Sam, the second to arrive, became tangled in the umbilical cord on his way out. The hot-dog doc had to literally unravel our youngest, boldly pulling Sam into life like a magician extricating the last gasping, freaked-out rabbit who's been accidentally suffocating in the top hat.

David laid our first boy on my chest: Ben was utterly calm, looking up at me. I was oblivious to everything else, exhausted, naturally, luxuriating in my first intimate moment with this fine-looking new specimen we'd been given, and trusting David would look after Sam. As predicted, the second delivery was not painful for me. But while we were waiting for Sam's arrival it began to dawn on David that something was amiss. Nobody said anything, but an extra, unfamiliar doctor had materialized next to the hot-dog doc, all eyes sober-looking and intent over surgical masks.

We'd asked Eliza's pediatrician, Jay, to be with us for the occasion, almost for comfort, like a touchstone. Jay quickly went over to David and began to whisper soothingly in his ear.

It's okay. It's okay. It's okay.

The boys had been lined up perfectly when my contractions started the night before, but somehow when Ben was working his way out past his brother, part of Sam's umbilical cord got tangled, wrapping him tightly in an extremely awkward, potentially lethal position, delaying his entrance long past the preferred time gap. Everything did turn out okay. But the hot dog was visibly shaken, and for Sam's father there was an excruciating interval of fear that our youngest might be *broken*.

All the short answers are installed and proofread and we're in the home stretch: uploading the long essay. Sam ended up bagging his *My Philosophy* idea, we discover, opting instead for a topic from Ivy U's list of suggestions: *a class or intellectual experience that has inspired you.* David hasn't had a chance to read it yet. Sam's written about a class taught by his favorite, most inspiring English teacher, keeping him anonymous. This teacher was fired late last year, and Sam, who has a strong tendency to stick up for underdogs, wants to protect him in case someone reads about the man's unorthodox, life-changing teaching style and decides not to hire him. Judging by my quick skim earlier this evening, it's a very appreciative, thoughtful essay and David wants to see.

It's 11:55 now. I'm so nervous that we're going to have something go wrong at midnight again but my husband, the father of our boys, has a right to savor his youngest offspring's last eloquent bid for the future before uploading.

David reads Sam's long essay. And indeed, he agrees it is acceptable. Lilly rests her nose on my foot.

Done. Submit.

Nothing Is Broken.

Our sons are on their way.

6.

Toy Story

Toy Story 3 has hit a major boomer nerve.

This movie is the highest-grossing Pixar film to date. It's even more successful than its predecessors, *Toy Story 1* and *2*; in fact it's the first animated feature film ever to hit the billion-dollar world-wide box-office mark. That callous little wretch Andy has grown up and abandoned his toys, and he's leaving for college exactly the same summer as Ben and Sam. This means we're right smack in the center of the Pixar target zone.

Toy Story is not the first movie to get under my parental skin like this. Back when the boys were just a couple of months old, David and I, exhausted, wanted to try a night out. We hadn't yet dared leave all three children at home with helpers, and I insisted we needed three for this maneuver, for safety's sake. We only had two sitters that I knew well enough to trust, so, crossing fingers, we took a leap of faith with a new one to make up a trio. Because I was breastfeeding, the outing required military-type planning—it took about a week to sock away enough extra breast milk to last for our two hours of freedom and get all my elaborate written instructions in shape for the three sitters. I think it was the newness of our third helper that got to me, although the breastfeeding theme in the movie David let me choose didn't help much.

Till then, I'd always enjoyed a good scary movie—I'd screamed enthusiastically through *Silence of the Lambs* the year before, clawing at David in delighted spasms. Now I was eager for another psychic release after the long postnatal confinement, so *The Hand that Rocks the Cradle*, starring Rebecca De Mornay as the malevolent nanny, seemed like a great idea. When we left the three sitters with all their instructions and refrigerated breast milk I was walking on air, finally out with my husband like a normal person. The good feeling began to dissipate just a little when De Mornay (secretly having a psychotic break due to a recent miscarriage) started giving the baby's mother mean looks behind her back. I tried my best to squelch images of Sitter Number Three back at home grabbing our butcher knife from the rack in the kitchen, offing numbers One and Two and then slowly, deliberately climbing the stairs, knife dripping, softly singsonging, *El-iiiii-za? Be-ennn? Sa-ammm?*

We made it all the way to that scene where De Mornay slithers into the baby's room to nurse it herself. Popcorn went flying, and I was out of there.

You'd think at this point I'd know it's best to avoid movies that are dangerously close to my emotional core. I can't help it, I'm a sucker for cinematic catharsis. And *Toy Story* is just a cartoon— right?

I've been investigating online. The general consensus seems to be that the *Toy Story* series is particularly meaningful to fathers. All the main characters are men. Original story credits for the trilogy are given to male writers only, and the opening date for this current installment was two days before Father's Day, Friday, June 10. Three days after our boys' high school graduation.

For some reason David and I ended up seeing *Toy Story 3* without our kids a couple of months ago. The Cineplex was packed with people of many shapes and sizes, and during the final wrenching scene, when Andy takes one last look at Woody, Buzz, Slinky Dog, and the gang from the window of his packed-up college-bound car at the end of the summer, I became aware of a throbbing mass of anguished adults literally keening all around us in the dark. I thought, *Now I know where my ABBA ladies have been hiding. And they've brought their husbands!*

There's been masculine outpouring online—grown men who haven't cried since they saw *Old Yeller* as kids are posting shamelessly, admitting they were blithering messes by the final good-bye.

An interesting paradox: Andy is fatherless, like many of the central characters in classic children's stories. The *Toy Story* writers are tight-lipped on the subject, but the online community has given it some thought. Most seem to agree that Andy's father died just before the first movie begins. They think Woody the cowboy (who's clearly a vintage '50s-era toy) must have belonged to Andy's dad originally, and represents a sort of paternal substitute, fretting alternately, as fathers do, between how best to do right by his son and how he and the gang will cope when his pal grows up and they're no longer needed.

They say these three movies represent archetypal stages of life. The first *Toy Story* is Youth. Woody is in his prime, full of innocent swagger. When space ranger Buzz Lightyear arrives, he's competition, and Woody reacts the way a particularly insecure parent might when confronted with his child's first inspiring middle school teacher or coach. And just as young navel-gazing boomer parents grapple with their own fallibility, the growing realization they can't shield their children from all the ills of the world no matter how hard they try, Buzz falls apart when he's forced to face the fact that he is only a toy, and not (as he believes at first) a superhero charged to protect the galaxy from evil Emperor Zurg, equipped with a jet-powered laser-shooting spacesuit.

Toy Story 2's life stage is Middle Age. Woody the cowboy is beginning to show signs of wear. His shooting arm damaged, Woody spends most of this second installment in the franchise trying to summon his earlier agility despite a useless appendage flopping flaccid at his side (totally phallic!). He goes through a genuine (albeit animated) midlife crisis when confronted with his roots: As it turns out, Woody was once the central character of a *Sputnik-era* western-themed TV puppet show called *Woody's Roundup*, and he almost abandons Andy and the gang to fly off and spend eternity where he thinks he'll be better appreciated, on display in a toy museum in Tokyo with his former co-stars, rather than face an uncertain destiny as Andy's useless, deteriorating one-time favorite toy.

Here's something David and I have decided: Woody's cute, long-lost sidekick horse marionette from the *Roundup*, named Bullseye, must have been designed using a rescued greyhound as inspiration. Lilly's equine bearing is part of what attracted me to the breed, and Bullseye's kind of like a dog in a horse costume. He's a ringer for Lilly—athletic and sensitive, desperate to please, and meltingly woebegone all at once. Like all rescue animals, Bullseye's clearly pining for a permanent place where he belongs, what the greyhound adoption associations call a Forever Home. I wanted to eat Bullseye up when I first saw him. Now I have Lilly.

This year's *Toy Story 3* is about Death; it explores our fear of mortality, old age, and retirement. In 3-D, no less! Andy is eighteen, he's never home, and the neglected toys are desperate for contact, reduced to figuring out a way to make a cell phone ring deep inside the toy chest, on the off chance Andy will pick them up for a second rummaging around for it. The toys just need a hug!

I can relate.

The million-dollar question (okay *billion-worldwide-dollar question*) is, *Which of the gang will be left out on the curb? Which in a box in the attic? And which will be donated, retired to dreaded Sunnyside Day Care?* (Sunnyside! Sounds and *looks* like one of those assisted-living chains. *Toy Story 3*'s Sunnyside Day Care turns out to be precisely as dismal as we aging boomers fear a senior living place could be, complete with a skilled nursing-type toy-repair center kitted out with duct tape, epoxy, and spare batteries.)

Ben and Sam ended up choosing schools in completely opposite directions. They seemed satisfied with their decisions and were looking forward to new adventures. It made sense to simplify college drop-offs by splitting the duties: David would fly with Ben to Texas, we decided, because I'd already visited his school. Then, David could recuperate from being poisoned due to his massive sensitivity to fast food and Texas air fresheners while I delivered Sam up north later in the week. (David's time is precious at the moment, and he needs his health. He'll be joining the cast of HBO's *Tremé* in October—they introduced his character over a few episodes in their first season, which filmed last spring. This year he'll be a regular character, which means he'll be down there from mid-fall to late spring. When he arrives he's got his work cut out for him finding a rental house with a yard for Lilly and so forth.)

I was looking forward to taking Sam to school. This would be my first chance to see his New England campus, one of the places David and Sam had hit together already during the hectic tour circuit the summer before. The whole plan seemed logical.

Except maybe not.

Fortunately, David seemed healthy when he came home from Texas, and I was pleased that he and Ben had had some good father-son time. But in the middle of the night a few days before my scheduled trip north with Sam, I woke to a God-awful sound I couldn't identify.

At first I thought this might be Lilly—greyhounds metabolize their food extremely fast (what else is new?). Until my greyhound consultant Linda O'Brien recommended a later dinner hour, when Lilly was fed too early her stomach emptied while she was asleep and she would start loudly retching this slimy bile substance all over the bedroom floor in the wee hours. I kept having to stagger out of bed when Lilly had one of these attacks, cursing unsympathetically, and shut her in the master bathroom just to protect the carpets, which, of course, meant Lilly would spend the rest of the night yelping through the door in absolute terror. *(She's leaving you! You'll never see her again! You're going to lose EVERYTHING!)* Having been there, done that with endless nights nursing sick children throughout our child-rearing years, I find I must draw the line when an animal (no matter how meltingly woebegone) interferes with my sleep.

This night Lilly was peaceful. Someone was upstairs in David's third-floor office making the strangest racket. He often goes up there if he has trouble sleeping, to work, run lines, or watch sports, and I thought, *Boy, is* that *a loud show.* Some ham actor was really chewing the scenery—I couldn't tell if the guy was howling with fake laughter or manufacturing melodramatic wails of misery. Whatever it was, like Ma's *NPR baboon program*, I was desperate to make it *STOP* so I could go back to sleep, and I went up to ask David to please turn down the sound a little.

The attic was dim and the TV screen dark when I peered between the banisters at the top of the stairs. A strange caterwauling was coming from a figure in the shadows: my husband.

The thing is, I carry on as if I'm the emotional hair trigger in this partnership, and David's the even-tempered macho man. But what I love most about my best friend and soul mate is that he is a living, breathing human. His gift, both as an actor and as a man, is that he owns up to the deepest, most hidden aspects of himself; the tender, true parts that many males in our society have been conditioned to squelch.

I'd been impressed, almost envious, of David's philosophical attitude when Eliza left. He seemed a little sad, but it was like he knew she'd be fine, that it was totally fitting for her to start making her way in the world. I've been determined to emulate David's level of maturity for the boys' launch, but as it turns out, I've been operating under a false impression. The inner David was an emotional time bomb, and the bomb exploded that night on the third floor of our house.

It took a while for him to calm down and explain coherently what had happened.

A dream:

David and our three kids are with a group of other parents and children on a cliff, thousands of feet above a freezing-cold torrential river. For some

*inexplicable dream reason, they all have no choice but to jump off this cliff
to certain death. I am not there.*

*Everyone's terrified. Children are squatting in puddles of cold water,
trying to prepare themselves for the frigid rapids below. Eliza is around
somewhere—she's screaming but David can't see her face.*

*He finds the boys. They are right at the edge of the precipice, looking
down, summoning courage. They're about twelve years old.*

Ben tells David he has a stomachache. He's always been prone to them.

*David hugs Sam from behind, and tells him, as deeply and fully as he
can, that he loves him—*

One second.

Eliza is *faceless* and *screaming*? That's *it*? No hug, no lingering
good-bye for his only daughter and firstborn? And come to think
of it: *I* am not *there*? Exactly where *am* I? Shirking responsibility
after twenty-one years of devoted stay-at-home martyrdom? *Me*?
What, am I blithely jetting off to early retirement somewhere?
Taking up trick riding in Tokyo with Bullseye the Woebegone
Doghorse?

I know I've seemed a little maxed-out lately after all the college
tours and applications and so forth, and it's true I didn't go with
David to drop off Ben. But I'd like to be thought of as someone
who'd make a point of showing up for the odd torrential freezing-
river-cliff good-bye.

Okay, I get it. This is a serious father-son dream—geared more
toward the *Toy Story* guys than the ABBA ladies. We are in Woody,
Buzz, and Andy territory here. The Morse females (along with

other minor supporting characters like Barbie, Bo Peep, and Mrs. Potato Head) are simply going to have to deal.

Then, David realizes his sons are on a kind of chute that will take them over the cliff. A few kids and another grown-up have flown down the chute ahead of them to die. David wants to stop Ben and Sam. He wants to go first, but everything is happening too fast. And so, down the boys go to their deaths, leaving David behind.

David says that's when his heart broke—almost more physically than emotionally. It felt frighteningly, clinically real, so real the shock of it actually woke him. Cracked with the pressure of love.

He was inconsolable. I could barely make out what he was saying, not sure if I should call 911 or just keep him talking to exorcise the dream. What David described feeling was intensely sweet—soul-crushing in its bittersweetness: wanting the boys to go and live their lives without the baggage of their father and his broken heart.

David had a rough relationship with his own father, who died unexpectedly back when our two boys were only beginning to toddle. Nothing had been resolved; there had never been much love or approval felt in either direction. His father was a charming man in many ways, but troubled, and like so many people, David has been determined to have a different sort of bond with his young.

That night, the one thing David kept repeating was this:

They'll never know how much I love them. They'll never, ever know.

I know our boys can tell their father loves them, and I told David, *Of course they know. How could they not?*

That's not what he meant. The point for David was that his disconnection with his own father was difficult. He's worked through a lot of it, but he remembers his younger self, the awkward youngster, the aimless teenager, and then the young man emerging as a husband and a father, as someone blocked. He had three sisters and a mother, all of whom he was close to, but no real male connection. As a result he was reserved, around men particularly, for quite a while—some interpreted his demeanor as shy, even hostile, neither of which was true. Having children, and especially boys, changed that.

The immediate trust and acceptance of our little guys allowed David the freedom to be truly himself—to have fun, make jokes, and talk about the serious stuff without risking judgment or rejection. As the boys grew, David was able to grow too, tapping into the confidence they gave him. Sam and Ben have no way of understanding the rich gift they've offered their father, and how grateful he is. And, David thinks, this is as it should be; it's fitting they start their lives without being weighed down by any burden or knowledge of the pain he feels letting go of the instruments of his healing.

There's a device the *Toy Story* movies employ to great effect: When a human child like Andy leaves a scene, the toys can walk and talk. They are constantly arguing and running around getting into all kinds of trouble, but they have a rule that's never broken. When the child returns, the toys automatically stop what they're doing and flop on the bed, shelf, or floor, inanimate—exactly as they

SUSAN MORSE

were when the child first left the room. There's often a close-up on Woody's face when Andy's around—his frozen smile has the slightest *soupçon de Tom Hanks*, who provides his voice—and the genius of Pixar is that somehow we know *exactly* what Woody's thinking.

This is what David's been doing: preserving the illusion, carrying bags from car to dorm room with good humor and a smile.

Like a classic boomer parent, whether it's a good thing or not (which is debatable—some say we boomers let our kids treat us like doormats), Woody reminds himself over and over throughout the trilogy that Andy comes first. And by the end of *Toy Story 3*, he finally sees that Andy appreciates this. *Promise to take good care of these guys,* Andy tells the little girl he's bequeathing his gang to. *They mean a lot to me. Woody is brave, kind, and smart. He'll never give up on you. He'll be there for you no matter what.*

Last June at the Cineplex, I'd lost it during an earlier scene: the climax of *Toy Story 3*. The toys have finally realized that Andy did not intentionally send them out to the curb with the trash—he wants them safe in the attic. Unfortunately, there's no chance to celebrate because they are all on a conveyor belt at the dump, tumbling together, headed for a gigantic furnace, and there's no way out. (David's dream chute!) Crazy, but Pixar really makes you believe all the toys are going to die.

What happens at this point is gloriously right: with seconds of life left, Woody and the gang all join hands. (Or hoofs, or paws, depending. In the case of the piggy bank, Hamm: trotters.) The

92

message is clear to me. The kids may be gone, and the end may be approaching, but still, there is something to hold: our spouses, our friends, our pets, our own aging parents, our jobs, our volunteer gigs—whatever it is, we have something.

I've scrapped the original plan to take Sam to New England alone. David will be coming with us this week—no discussion. Next on the agenda: find an allergy-free room at the Marriott.

David, Sam, and Ben, 1993

7.

Releasing

A text message from Ben in Texas:

Mama guess what: It's really hot here and I always wear flip-flops, but while I was waiting at the bus stop near my dorm, all these little bugs climbed onto my feet and bit me. I tried to wipe them off but I think their heads were stuck inside my skin, because when I went to dinner I started feeling itchy all over and my throat was kind of closing up. But don't worry because when I got back to my room I took a Zyrtec and called the 24-hour nurse hotline. I think they're going to give me an EpiPen! Anyway, it's really hot, so is it fine if I buy some more shorts?

They're gone.

I'm determined to keep the wallowing to a minimum this time.

The boys' colleges don't hold freshman parents' hands at drop-off quite the same way Eliza's had: I had to find my own souvenir mugs from their campus stores, but I haven't been weeping into my breakfast tea—at least, not as regularly. Thanksgiving is coming. Mostly, I watch David. So far so good.

The experts tell parents with freshly emptied nests that it's best to keep moving. Here's a typical checklist:

- Exercise! Now's your chance to get in shape. Try something new! (There's a Zumba class up on the avenue, and my friend Rose has set up a group for her birthday next month. *Check.*)
- Travel! (First-rate house sitter installed on the premises. David will be heading down to New Orleans very soon to start work on *Tremé* and scout out Lilly-oriented living quarters. *Check.*)
- Communication! Every day there's a whole new technological way to stay in touch with your college kids. (New Skype account: *Check.* Cell phone by my side at all times: *Check.* Sign up for Facebook: *Check.*)

Honest, I'm not on Facebook to spy on my children. My friend Amy got me to sign up because it's a promotion tool for writers. Eliza is my Facebook friend, but I think she gave me restricted status because I never see anything even remotely juicy. I'm friends with Ben, but he never seems to post—he tells me boys aren't big on Facebook. I'm sure that's why my friend request to Sam has gone unanswered all these months.

My friend Martha just finished her first empty-nester year. Martha and her husband, John, have quite a spread: their eldest son, Roger, left for college twelve years ago, and their youngest, Philip, took off last year, so John and Martha are old hands. Martha says college boys generally don't make contact unless they actually need something, and I mustn't take their silence personally. Some kids need their space for a while.

I have another friend, Barbara, a shrink. Barbara still has a few children at home, and she's been plotting. When the last ones move out, Barbara wants to become an internist for Doctors Without Borders. Barbara says her motives are not entirely pure—she's stir crazy having stayed put all her adult life and would like to see something of the world before she's too old to travel. But mainly, Barbara says, she's pretty sure the only way she can stop herself from being a helicopter parent to her soon-to-be adult children will be to relocate entirely, preferably to a third-world country where cell phones and e-mails are not an option.

Is it too late for medical school?

Another tip from Martha: Take time to adjust. If at all possible, don't make drastic changes to your living situation right away. This makes perfect sense to me.

I love our home, and I'm still amazed we've pulled off that move from the West Coast. Networking is supposedly the key to success in the entertainment industry, and that's not possible in

Philly. Somehow David's always found enough work to keep us comfortably afloat far from show business hubs in New York and Los Angeles, and we feel very lucky we don't need to downsize now in order to pay for college. While I do have a degree of guilt about the energy waste of a semioccupied six-bedroom house, we are happy here and the thought of a move is depressing. We'll make changes, but none that affect the children too much just yet; I need them to know they're still welcome.

I have a house-wide carpet cleaning scheduled thanks to Lilly's nighttime bile eruptions, and because she also took a while to figure out where the dog bathroom was located, especially when I was not at home. Once she got the hang of the stairs, Lilly would go up there looking for me and, not finding me, relieve herself out of sheer frustration. Downstairs we have a sort of skylit greenhouse area you have to pass through on the way to the family room. It's paved in slate, flanked by giant fig trees David gave me for Mother's Day one year, and every time Lilly went through there looking for me she must have thought she was going outdoors, and assumed that the carpeted family room on the other side was where she was supposed to take care of business. She is clearly intelligent, always watching me, figuring out what's expected of her and synthesizing this new knowledge with lessons from her past life, so I think Lilly is past the messy phase. We are definitely due for a carpet overhaul, but I'm waiting till David's safely in New Orleans. We save potentially allergy-triggering household procedures for when he won't be around. Because he'll be home for Thanksgiving and Christmas, the fall will pass quickly, so we've decided I'll take care of administrative business up here, postponing my own drive south with Lilly till January when the kids are all back at college.

The children's rooms are their jurisdiction. I've pretty much felt at peace with keeping my nose out until a recent tour of Martha's home. Martha has a strong interest in interior design, and it shows. She and John live in an early twentieth-century stone house similar to and not far from ours. I cannot figure out what they have done with their junk—there is nothing showing anywhere. Was it like that before their children left? Even the bedrooms are impeccable. How does she do it?

Our kids chose their colors years ago. In Sam's and Ben's rooms, honking neon yellow walls clash with moss-green carpets, but what distinguishes their areas most particularly is the colossal amount of boy-crap. It's best to keep their doors closed. I did tiptoe in earlier this week to haul out several loads of garbage (half-empty water bottles, crumpled chip bags, mummified marshmallow Peeps still nestled in forgotten Easter baskets—interestingly, the condoms the Easter Bunny put in last year's baskets seem to be missing).

I've determined it's not quite necessary to fumigate, but even with most of the hazardous waste removed, every surface is covered—snarls of unidentifiable charger cords; teetering pick-up-stick towers of dried felt markers and broken pencil stubs; vast mountain ranges of books. Mantels jammed with mismatched souvenirs from David's film locations: tiny bearskin-hatted Buckingham guards standing sentry by leering, furry-haired Swedish trolls.

I've asked my fastidious friend Martha how she maintains order. Did she perform major purges herself, after each boy left? Or did she ask them to get rid of their own junk when they packed, and if so, how was this accomplished without threats and violence? Martha says their boys' tidiness was mostly self-motivated. She'd simply point out the shortage of spare hangers once a year or so. Roger and Phillip would leap promptly into action, and a discreet, manageable assortment of discarded clothing and toys would appear in the hall.

For my boys, clothes hangers are obsolete medieval artifacts. Ben and Sam would laugh at me. *Who needs hangers with all this great floor space?*

Maybe I should have apologized in advance to their roommates.

I've found a good distraction for David. This week he's been kind enough to help with the heavy-lifting phase of our only significant household change: the computer room is becoming my new office.

The concept behind the computer room was based on parenting experts' advice that children's risky Internet activity should take place in an open common area. Our kids' workroom is an airy space, stationed strategically on the ground floor. This location provided me with plenty of pretexts to breeze through pretending not to check up on them, which helped the children develop spectacular hand-eye coordination—they became quite skilled at switching off those screens whenever they heard me coming.

The computer room had originally been the study for the former master of the house, and when we moved here we installed enough countertop for three computer stations. There's a glass cabinet of shelves stocked with supplies (paper, poster board, modeling clay, glue) and a deep closet under the stairs filled with communal toys: board games, train sets, costumes, and least-favorite stuffed animals. All our kids were stuffie lovers. They still have wicker chests filled with special favorites in their bedrooms. I think I'll let the children decide their stuffies' fates—I haven't yet recovered from the tragic demise of a little fluffy white toy rabbit when I was four. As the family's financial manager, and because I began writing more and more as the kids got older, I've been lusting after the computer room's prime location. David has helped me cart down my file cabinets. Next I'm going to reclaim the closet space.

The front hall is now stacked waist-high with boxes hauled out from under the computer-room stairs: a vast collection of matchbox cars; a large dress-up bin overflowing with purple feathery boas, rainbow clown wigs, and little-bitty Batman capes; dozens of never-used birthday craft kits; an ancient, flattened Monopoly set from my childhood, barely held together at the corners with dried-out masking tape. Several decks of "W" playing cards: our former president's beaming face Photoshopped onto an assortment of 1940s pinup girls (George in a tutu; George on a bearskin rug; George at the beach, spilling out of his halter top).

Quite a workout, going through all this stuff and deciding what to do with everything. The activity wakes my circulation and even cheers me a bit, although it's a little upsetting for Lilly. *(You can't lie down close to her, there's too much in the way. It's exhausting.)* I keep having to wrestle with an exuberant tunnel that refuses to behave—

twenty feet of blue canvas stretched around a giant spring that keeps exploding, like Snakes-in-a-Can, causing Lilly to dive for cover.

Mostly, I'm in denial about the castle.

We found this Fisher-Price Great Adventures Castle at a Toys"R"Us in Maine the summer after the earthquake, when David was filming *The Langoliers* at Bangor International Airport. It has everything three-year-old boys could have wished for back then: a moat and drawbridge, trapdoors capping each turret, and a fully functional cannon on the balcony. For years the castle occupied center stage in a bedroom Ben and Sam shared. It was such a favorite we kept going back for more accessories over several years: an add-on Boulder Blaster for hurling plastic rocks; a giant dragon-shaped Arrow Shooter on wheels. Each addition came with a fresh installment of little knights with moveable arms, brandishing swords, axes, flails, and shields.

I've been keeping the knights in a storage box from Kmart, and it may be my imagination, but I could swear they're glowering at me now through the clear plastic lid. I get the impression my sons' tiny warriors aren't bothered much by Woody and Buzz's *Toy Story 3*–type retirement anxiety. These chaps are professional soldiers, and something tells me if the lady of the house is plotting their disposal, they won't go down without a fight.

No. I have to be ruthless, like Martha. Everything must go. I actually believe I mean this, and the horror of my decision evokes an instant real-life flashback, like an extremely effective acting "sense memory" exercise: *I am about four years old. I've been sleeping with Fluffy Bunny every night for so long he's almost a part of my body. I'm in the bathroom at a friend's house, and . . . Nooooo, Fluffy Bunny just toppled into the unflushed toilet. I'm going to die.*

I retreat to the kitchen for Kleenex, trying not to inflict myself on David, who's fixing his breakfast. His cell chirps. Another text from Ben!

Hi Papa, I don't want you to worry but can you check what CNN is saying? We're in lockdown, there's a bunch of SWAT guys with a tank outside the window, and they told us to sit here on the floor in a corner of the classroom. So that's what we're doing, but we're just wondering if they've caught the campus shooter yet. And how's everything at home?

Well, *that* gets the adrenaline flowing. We spend the next hour watching CNN clips of the action on campus, and updating Ben. Shots have been fired; no injuries reported, and we're relieved to hear his girlfriend, Jilli, is now safe in her dorm after being caught in an every-man-for-himself-type stampede on her way to class. Jilli's been wearing an orthopedic boot because of a stress fracture—not entirely convenient when making a fast getaway. She says she could actually see the tip of the guy's gun barrel bobbing above masses of panic-stricken students running every which way. Lovely.

CNN runs out of information to report, and they fill the time by pointing out the iconic UT clock tower, which, as it turns out, was once the setting of a historic campus shooting I'd never heard of: back in 1966, an ex-Marine enrolled at Ben's college went on a rampage, killing thirteen people and injuring more before he was gunned down on the clock tower's observation deck by an Austin police officer.

Why did nobody mention that on the tour?

Nothing we can do but wait and see how this unfolds. Ben signs off, agreeing to keep us posted, and David heads out to the gym.

How can he just leave at a time like this? I inherited a fierce disaster complex from my father, and for some unknown reason David doesn't always feel the need to participate. I turn the volume up so I can keep track of things, and try to resume my sorting project in the hall. I think Lilly can tell something's up. She refuses to settle and keeps trying to pick her way through all the rubble to get closer to me.

The kids don't even know we have all this stuff. There are plenty of memories in their ~~hell holes~~ *bedrooms. We'll only keep the grown-up games. Anything for children will go.*

Jilli has younger brothers, I remember, and her family lives nearby. I decide to make two separate piles: one for donations and one for Jilli's guys.

From their tangle in the open box, the grim little Fisher-Price knights regard me warily, eyes obscured by visors and helmets. I could swear one of them just tightened the grip on his cudgel, and my heart goes out to him, bless his little plastic about-to-go-down-the-toilet-like-Fluffy-Bunny soul. I know I'm projecting pointlessly on inanimate objects; I can't help it. My children are frigging gone, out there being shot at and stuff, and there's nothing I can do. What *else* can I project on, the *dog*? Never mind. I can handle this empty nest. At the moment I have a terrible surging impulse to zip open my womb and stuff every last one of these little Fisher-Price buggers inside—castle, Boulder Blaster and all, like a reverse C-section—but give me a second. I'm sure this feeling will pass.

It's Pixar's fault. *Toy Story* is creating a generation of hoarders.

The phone rings and I climb over everything to find it—Sam.

—I need to transfer.

—You need to what?

—Do you think I can transfer out of here in January?

—Sam. Are you talking about this year?

—Yeah.

—You want to transfer second semester of your *freshman year*?

It turns out Sam is not taking well to his new school for all kinds of reasons. He's been talking to friends having the opposite experience, and Sam is hell-bent on switching. We have a brief, charged discussion, mostly me talking, lecturing about not making snap decisions, giving things time, and how I managed to weather early vapors at boarding school.

I must remind myself: academics are only one piece of the pie chart of a young person's college education. Released from home, they finally have the chance to solve their own problems without parental interference. I manage to hold on to this one rational thought for maybe ninety seconds, and then surrender, abandoning the hall mess again, Lilly scrambling ahead of me—*Lilly, I love you, but MAN, you are so up my ASS you are making me NUTS*—and I jab around on the Internet, download a map of Ben's campus hoping to figure out exactly where he's holed up, and simultaneously Google "transfer application guidelines" for Sam. The phone rings again.

Eliza has fallen prey to a speed trap near her off-campus apartment in Virginia, a state where going thirty miles per hour in a twenty-five zone is the equivalent of holding up a convenience store.

—Bad luck. Now you'll have to drive like a granny.

—Like *Granny*?

—No! If you drive like Granny they'll take your license. Drive like *a* granny, a *normal* one—I don't care how many drivers get mad at you, just let them honk. Try not to break one single traffic law from now till you leave Virginia.

Perfect: Sam's going to drop out and live under a bridge for the rest of his life, Eliza is one step away from a criminal record, and Ben, as long as he hasn't gone into anaphylactic shock since last time I checked, is on national television, dodging the unspeakable.

CNN drones. Ben's campus is apparently still in lockdown, although the gunman has been neutralized, whatever that means. I wait for another text. A phrase flits into my consciousness—can't remember where it comes from: *You are only as happy as your least happy child.*

Life moves too fast. Do I have to let *everything* go? Isn't there a compromise?

Lilly tiptoes over and puts her head on my knee.

Okay, how about this: grown-up-type games everyone likes can be salvaged, but I know that's only a practical concession. I'm seeking comfort. The children's important memories are in their rooms already, buried under a ton of crap, admittedly, but most of their personal treasures are up there for them to deal with as they please. They don't care about what's down here—*I'm* the one who cares, and this sudden admission pricks me with intense relief. What's to stop me from sparing a few small tokens from this collection, just for myself? Does that count as wallowing? My new office closet under the stairs is huge, after all. There has to be room.

For me: One mangled headdress. It's in a photo I treasure: knobby-kneed Ben in rubber cowboy boots dashing through the house.

For me: One tiny black hooded sweatshirt—I trimmed it painstakingly with white faux fur Fluffy Bunny stripes the year Eliza wanted to be a skunk for Halloween.

For me: One glittery jester hat, from another favorite moment—Sam leaning into the curve on an amusement-park ride; flying, blissful, twinkling jingle-bell tips streaming behind.

And the knights. Yes. For me: the knights can stay.

8.

Sleep Disorder

Back to that empty-nest checklist:

* Romance! Whether you're already in a relationship or
  on the lookout for one, who's to stop you now from spicing things up a little?

Hmmmm . . . what exactly do they have in mind? Naughty
underwear? Sex toys? Maybe a round of couples' swinging with
some of the ABBA ladies and their *Toy Story* guys?

If there truly are aliens somewhere in the outer stratosphere, using special extraterrestrial camera probes that beam through the walls and ceilings of our homes and monitor Earthling behavior, I hope they haven't been focusing too much on the Morse master bedroom. We're not typical.

Curtain up: A bedroom in shadows. Two lumps in the bed: one large and male, one slightly smaller and female. A blade-thin greyhound sleeps on the floor by the female lump's side of the bed, next to a tabletop cluttered with a teetering pile of books, and a spray bottle. A digital alarm clock reads 3:27 a.m. Stillness.

The dog lets out a little high-pitched REM-state yip. The male lump stirs.

MALE LUMP. *(Softly)* Ell.

Silence. The male lump twitches. The dog yips again and pedals her legs spastically, chasing a dream rabbit.

MALE LUMP. *(A little louder)* Ell. Ell Eee.

The female lump stirs slightly.

FEMALE LUMP. Mrr?

MALE LUMP. *(Very loud, twitching a lot)* ESS-ESS!!!! ELL EEE! ELL EEE!

FEMALE LUMP. Okay.

The male lump continues to twitch. The dog continues to pedal and yip. The female lump rolls over and scrabbles on the bedside table, causing most of the books to fall and land on the dog, who startles and jumps to her feet.

FEMALE LUMP.   S^&#.

MALE LUMP.   ELL EEE! ELL EEE! ELP!

FEMALE LUMP.   I know, I know you need help. I'm on it. I'm trying to get the damn water thingy—

MALE LUMP.   ELLLLLLP!

FEMALE LUMP.   *(Waving the spray bottle)* Got it.

The dog is now pacing back and forth at the foot of the bed, panting anxiously. The female lump squirts her bottle in the air a couple of times to get the thing going, then reaches over and sprays the male lump once on the shoulder.

FEMALE LUMP.   How's that? Lilly, go back to sleep.

MALE LUMP.   *(Still twitching)* O.

FEMALE LUMP.   Shoot. Okay. Um, let me think.

MALE LUMP.   ELP! ELLLPP!!!

FEMALE LUMP.   Okay, okay, okay. On the head. Ready?

She squirts him three times in rapid succession on the side of the head, hard. The male lump suddenly bolts upright.

MALE LUMP.   Damn! Right in my ear.

FEMALE LUMP.   Sorry. Okay?

MALE LUMP.   Yes. Darn. Thank you.

FEMALE LUMP.   Okay.

MALE LUMP.   Sorry.

FEMALE LUMP.   Okay. Lilly, lie down.

They go back to sleep. Lights fade on Lilly, standing by the bed, watching them, statue-dog.

The doctors call it narcolepsy. We call it Waking-Up Attacks.

Waking-Up Attacks have been going on for decades. I think they're becoming more and more resistant, like a stubborn virus. David says what happens is his throat collapses, and it's terrifying, like being buried alive. He sort of wakes up, but he's mostly paralyzed. He can't really do anything about his collapsed throat—similar to those dreams where you try to run away from something but your legs won't work and you keep falling down. He needs to wake up so he can open his airway and breathe, but for some reason this strapping six-foot-four, two-hundred-plus-pounder has a really hard time achieving total consciousness without outside help.

Back in our heady, romantic early days, David was easy to wake—I'd just say his name and he'd snap out of it. Then one night came the first warning that the mystery was gone and our relationship would be settling into a dangerous stretch. I knew the signs of a budding Waking-Up Attack well by then, and at his first little *Elp!* I said, *David. David? David! Wake up!* but he kept right on twitching. So I tried giving him a little poke, which solved the problem.

Over time, poking became less and less effective, and my poke evolved into a sort of shove. Then the shove had to keep getting more and more aggressive in order to work, all building up to one pivotal night when I found myself lurching on top of David into a straddle position and bouncing up and down, making the bedposts rattle. This tactic (one might assume) could add enough spice to satisfy any empty-nester checklist. Under our circumstances, it definitely did not. I think this is when I began to speculate about alien spies picking us as random subjects for Earthling behavior research, and David, fearing bodily injury, suggested the spray bottle.

The spray bottle was a stroke of genius—it's worked for years now. I keep a spare in my travel bag.

When I'm not around, David can be trapped in Waking-Up Attack state for ages until he finally twitches himself into consciousness. (He had one on a plane once. Oddly, David is sometimes able to see what's going on around him even though he can't really function. He says he could tell the surrounding passengers were watching, probably figuring he was drunk or something, and then turning away embarrassed, as if to give him his space. This could not have been easy, given all David's flopping around.) Often he hallucinates, thinking I'm there when I'm not. He'll incorporate me into his dream, becoming more and more frustrated. He thinks he can see me, and can't understand why I won't wake up and spray him so he can go back to sleep.

I find David's adaptive resistance to my Waking-Up Attack strategies intriguing. There's definitely an analogy that could be applied, to do with the hazards of over-familiarity in marriage— something to consider at this turning point in our domestic life. One very significant factor we've identified is that if he has any reason to suspect I'm annoyed at the interruption to my sleep, I don't have to lift a finger. Guilt wakes David immediately.

The thing is, I am never annoyed. Okay, maybe occasionally, but I know my husband is not having Waking-Up Attacks on purpose just to inconvenience me. We're all aware that maintaining a successful long-term relationship requires schooling yourself to see things from your mate's perspective. David deserves credit for being tolerant of what he calls my Sleep Kicking. I fall asleep curled in a considerate little fetal ball, but at some point in the night I need to unfold, explosively, like a well oiled jackknife, causing my feet to unexpectedly sock him right in the kidneys.

Imagine the problems we'd solve if we could find a way to have my Sleep Kicking coincide with David's Waking-Up Attacks.

He's had three sleep studies—you spend the night in a hospital, covered with sensors so they can monitor you—but to date, the only people who have ever witnessed one of David's Waking-Up Attacks in all its glory are those embarrassed seatmates on the plane, and me. After one study, the doctor told David to bring me along for the big final meeting to discuss the results. This sort of worried me—David's perfectly capable of making his own medical decisions. What did they need me for?

Apparently they had picked up just enough activity to diagnose a mild case of narcolepsy, which, according to *Wikipedia*, is *a neurological disorder caused by the brain's inability to regulate sleep-wake cycles normally*. A main characteristic of narcolepsy is *excessive daytime sleepiness*. It comforted me greatly to know this, because I'd been feeling a little sensitive on date nights. I have enough trouble eating in public with a recognizable actor. When that actor nods off center stage at a candlelit table for two before the appetizers arrive, it's humiliating.

Another classic symptom seemed accurate to David. It's called *lucid dreaming*. This is where you're awake and dreaming at the same time, which is the crux of David's experience. He realizes what's happening, and wakes just enough to know he needs my attention, but not quite enough to be able to do anything concrete to help himself. *Hypnagogic hallucination* is common as well—this is where you're sort of semiconscious, and you see and hear things that aren't there. I've been brooding on this particular feature of narcolepsy ever since David had a Waking-Up Attack as I was coming out of the bathroom one night. He was positive I was still in the bed—he says he could actually see me sleeping beside him. Unfortunately, still in the middle of an unusually intense dream, he was particularly jumpy. So when I crossed the room to help, approaching from an unexpected angle, David, who must have perceived me to be some sort of home-invasion threat, sprang instantly out of bed in action-ninja mode (all two hundred-plus pounds of him) and seized my wrist in a vise-grip.

Aside from scaring the crap out of me, what's particularly intriguing is that a variation of this idiosyncratic trait is also commonly associated with greyhounds.

The rescue people warned us it's a bad idea to startle a sleeping greyhound. Other than wanting to chase (and possibly eat) small, cute animals, aggression is not much of an issue with these dogs, except when they are asleep. A lot of them will deliver a warning nip (or worse) if you try to pet them when they're resting. It's hard to say if this is a breed-specific characteristic or simply a side effect of early kennel life, where each racing dog sleeps alone, undisturbed in its own private crate.

For some reason Lilly is not normally fazed by interference while sleeping, which is lucky for us. I first realized we'd dodged this one bullet when we heard from Eliza in Florida last summer. Caught up in our household's consuming greyhound fever, Eliza decided to spend a good chunk of her vacation between junior and senior year at college embedded at a greyhound rescue farm, helping out with chores in exchange for direct access, research for a self-designed art fellowship: a documentary about the life of a typical racing dog from birth to retirement. A heroine of the rescue movement, Grace, kindly took Eliza in for a month's stay at her compound. Freshly retired greyhounds spend their first weeks with Grace before being assigned to foster homes on the path to adoption.

Grace has devoted her life to greyhound rescue. Her kennel is always filled to capacity with recent refugees awaiting transfer, and it breaks her heart if she can't take every single dog from the tracks in her area. Those that can't be placed due to serious health conditions, Grace keeps, sharing her own limited living quarters with at least a dozen grateful misfits—greyhounds with seizure disorders; greyhounds with only three legs, one lost due to an accident in their last race, a death sentence without Grace's intervention. Whenever I feel particularly exasperated by my one clingy dog, I think of Grace and her Mother Teresa lifestyle and I feel like a wimp.

There were about fifteen of these lucky rejects living with Grace in her double-wide trailer last summer when Eliza stayed there for one hot, unforgettable month. Eliza was assigned to the guest room, which was surprisingly comfortable for a trailer, except that on her first night, a pair of mostly adorable whippets named Abbott and Costello made it clear she would not be sleeping alone.

David and I have enough trouble sleeping with each other—beds and sofas are off limits to Morse dogs. Like many diehard dog lovers, Grace enforces no particular furniture policy. Abbott and Costello had established the guest bed as their sleeping quarters long before Eliza's arrival, so she had to get used to them burrowing under the covers on either side of her while she was catching up on e-mails in the evenings. This was tricky because if Eliza so much as cleared her throat, one or the other of these little buggers, true to the characteristics of their breed, would rouse immediately, growling and snapping. So our princess spent a lot of sleepless nights not daring to even lean over and switch off her reading light—a character-building kind of summer.

It eventually became clear why David's sleep doctor wanted me at that consultation session. We went over the diagnosis, and David rejected the offer of heavy-duty uppers and downers to keep him regulated. Then I was handed a pamphlet showing one remaining option. David and the doctor watched me carefully.

I opened to the first illustration: a couple in bed.

Talk about spicing things up. Not exactly what I had in mind in the way of sex toys.

I really did try to keep a straight face.

Curtain up: A bedroom in shadows. Two lumps in the bed: one large and male, one slightly smaller and female. Both are sleeping peace-fully. Most of the male lump's face is covered by an elaborate system of Velcro straps securing a monstrous gas mask. A wide, elephantine, almost pulsating opaque tube snakes ominously from the center of the mask (roughly where the male lump's nose might be) to a pump-type gadget hissing rhythmically on the nightstand.

David hates the mask even more than I do. We keep it in the attic, and muddle along with our spray bottle, hoping for the best.

9.

The SBDs

She says, "Watch the house, Lilly, I'll be back." And she closes it.

You wait.

You're not hungry now, but you will be. You need to SEE her.

If you had more of us with you, you'd be safe. But none of us is here. Only you.

Oh, please, where is she? You want her BAAAACK, and you hope she's on the other side, so jump up there and see. Just jump, now!

Oh, it's so high and slippery, you can't stay here. This is not good. Call her! COME BACK! COME BAAAAAAACK! BAAAAACK!

Maybe she's here, like when you're sleeping and you wake up and you go find her. It's so big in this place, she could be anywhere. Could she have come in another way? Keep looking, everywhere, everywhere. Oh, you

can't stop panting, and you're so thirsty. Everywhere, look everywhere,
COME BAAAAAAACK!

This is not the place, but you have to do it, you can't help it, it's com-
ing out, oh, here it comes. COME BAAAAAACK! BAAAAACK BACK BACK
BAAAAAACK!!!

Go to where she closed it, and try your teeth. It hurts, you're so tired but
too bad, you have to keep trying.
COME BAAAAAAAAAACK.

Here's the thing. David and I have been under surveillance for decades. We've never seen them, but I'm positive they're out there. If I were really clever, I'd put them to work—they could take out the trash, maybe, or keep Lilly company so she doesn't freak when I have to leave.

At first I thought they were crouching in the shrubs outside our kitchen window. Eventually, I came to suspect they were also employing sophisticated equipment to tap our phones and e-mail correspondence. It's not exactly clear whether their long-term goal is to preserve our family or destroy it. I have my theories. What I do know for sure is they have superb connections in the entertainment industry. This is why we call them the Show Business Demons, or, informally, the SBDs.

The SBDs are disturbingly skilled at ruining things. Their specialty: Securing Inconvenient Out-of-Town Job Offers for David— the lengthier the better, right when something important is happening. When a child is born, say, or we're packing for a move or there's some special parent event at school.

Looking back, I now believe it was SBDs who almost wrecked our Philadelphia wedding in 1982. David and I were so gullible in the early days. We were based in New York at the time—although David was mostly in L.A., just beginning a new television series called *St. Elsewhere*. We wanted a traditional ceremony at my parents' church in Philadelphia, and when we discovered there was a generous, iron-clad three-week gap in David's shooting schedule right at the start of my summer break from acting class in New York, we thought: *Perfect*. David could spend his break in New York with me, allowing plenty of time to get the license in Philly, make other preparations, and finally tie the knot on a Saturday in late June. We might even grab a quick honeymoon somewhere nice before spending the rest of the summer together on the West Coast while he was filming.

The innocence! It never even occurred to us how laughably naïve we were not to anticipate the multitude of things that could and would go wrong, from the moment I committed us to the June date by slipping all those stamped, hand-addressed invitations in a mailbox on the corner of Ninth Avenue and Fifty-First Street. We were not yet acquainted with the SBDs, who started with one of their simplest tactics: Screwing with the Production Schedule.

Sorry, David's producers said. *The hospital set looks a little dark on film, and we need to recast two key characters. We're going to reshoot the pilot. No June break.*

No problem, David told me on the phone. *St. Elsewhere* didn't have him on the schedule that last Monday before the wedding. Back then you needed a blood test to get married, so David would get his done in L.A., he said, then fly to New York on Sunday and hop on a train to grab the license with me at Philadelphia's City Hall. Then he'd fly back to L.A. for a few more days of filming and be back in Philly with plenty of time to prepare for the rehearsal dinner and the wedding.

Deftly, the SBDs shifted to one of their favorite ploys: Loss of Vital Documents.

We still didn't smell a rat when David arrived in New York, looked through his bags, and couldn't find his blood-test results. *No problem*, my parents said, and they set us up with a doctor friend who could perform a quickie test in Philly on Monday morning. Blood test in hand, off we went to City Hall.

Which, we discovered on arrival, was closed.

Here's a little-known bit of Philly trivia: Pennsylvania is the only state in our union that observes an obscure public holiday in June called Flag Day. Hardly anybody around here acknowledges Flag Day as far as I can tell—just random public institutions like post offices and the Department of Motor Vehicles—so it's quite easy to live in Philadelphia for years without even realizing this holiday exists. Flag Day has something to do with Betsy Ross, we've been told, but I know better. Flag Day is an SBD tactic, proof that they've been at this a very long time—I'm guessing they put Betsy Ross on the payroll way back in 1776. *The Morses will be marrying in June of 1982,* they told her. *We'll need an Unanticipated Closure of Public Buildings around then, so please be sure you finish sewing that flag by the end of May.*

We left City Hall empty-handed and David had to fly back to L.A. on a red-eye that night. He still had one other day off before the wedding, allowing just barely enough time to squeeze in a second round-trip to Philly for the license, returning that night to L.A. for work on Thursday, and finally, grabbing a third flight Friday morning for our rehearsal dinner. After Ping-Ponging back and forth across the country six times in five days, when David headed down the church aisle that Saturday in his seersucker wedding duds, he could barely walk straight.

I was in love—so young and foolish—flattered by my gallant groom's determination to claim his bride. I thought we were simply living a charming real-life romantic comedy. The SBDs must have been laughing their scaly little asses off.

Sometimes we appreciate their humor. Sometimes we don't. David missed the funerals of both his father *and* his stepfather.

It's a kind of lifelong sporting event. We've tried various strategies over the years—for a while we made plans very loudly, in backwards code:

—*Susan, I've got the dates for the Lars von Trier movie in Sweden this summer. When do you want to bring the kids?*

—*Um . . . I don't know. They're pretty busy this summer. What are the dates?*

—*Well, the producer told me they could put us in a house on a beautiful lake in June.*

—*A house on a lake? David, why would we want to stay in a house on a lake? I mean, who cares about lakes?*

—*You're right. I'm sorry, it's just I've been away a lot and I miss everyone. I know it won't be any fun. All they have is boring ponies and sheep there, sort of wandering around right outside the house. And they say the owner will take the* kids out in his boat to catch trout, and he shows them how to smoke it, and then everyone eats freshly smoked trout for dinner that the kids caught themselves.

—Oh, I HATE smoked trout. And June will NEVER work. School is over the first week in June, which means if you have them book us on a flight to Sweden for JUNE TENTH, the kids will be REALLY DISAPPOINTED, because I have just this minute found a TENNIS CAMP starting that exact week. They would NEVER agree to pass up on a once-in-a-lifetime chance to go to tennis camp just so they can ride dumb ponies and fish for trout on some HORRIBLE, ICKY LAKE in Sweden. So whatever you do, don't book us a flight for JUNE TENTH. In fact, as soon as we hang up, I am going to call and sign them up for TENNIS CAMP the week of JUNE TENTH.

—Got it. June tenth.

June 1999, Gothenburg

The SBDs just kept compensating. They formed a new specialty unit, which has become their signature: Orchestration of Inconvenient Last-Minute Weather and Health Glitches. Children developed sudden fevers the Friday night before a trip to visit David on location. Air travel was unexpectedly shut down by ice storms in April. I'd call the airlines, trying futilely to change flights, picturing SBDs out there in our bushes or wherever they were, high-fiving a job well done. Pouring buckets of Gatorade over everyone's heads and slapping one another on their creepy hunchbacks.

When I was acting as well, in the times BC, I spent a lot of time on David's sets, because there was so much to learn. It was a real thrill to watch shows being filmed, at first. After a while the slow pace can get to you—sort of like a baseball game, with long hours waiting between camera setups, punctuated by quick flurries of action, and then more waiting. Nothing to do but eat snacks laid out at the craft-services table and make small talk with whoever else is standing around. It's the small talk that gets me in trouble.

I try to avoid the famous people on set because of my terrible Lucy Ricardo tendency to embarrass Ricky by sticking my fat foot in my mouth. This happened more and more when my focus shifted to the kids and I wasn't getting out much. I have trouble connecting faces with names, and often I'd be introduced to some huge celebrity and have no clue who they were. I once asked Lloyd Bridges if he had any kids, and he looked at me like, *What* is your *problem?* Another time, after talking all evening to an interesting guy named Charlie, very struck by his commanding presence, I began to wonder what he did for a living. Fortunately I had enough of my wits about me to whisper my question in David's ear before asking "Charlie" point-blank if he was maybe the movie's producer or something. Oops. Charles Bronson. Playing David's father in the movie. Right, I knew that.

Even when I was still working, I was a hazard; busting into a wardrobe trailer uninvited to glimpse George C. Scott in his underdrawers right in the middle of a fitting; flashing my own undies at Henry Winkler outside the Emmys—David and I were just walking over to say hi, and a breeze lifted my flimsy silk wraparound skirt completely over my head. I encountered him again at an audition once and, of course, had to relive my mortification by telling the story to a roomful of bored executives. (Henry claimed he'd completely forgotten.)

After I stopped working, I'd bring the children so they could be with their father during holidays, and with my focus on them, I managed to stay out of trouble. On the odd occasion when I've been by myself in the galaxy where David works, I feel like a party crasher. David usually helps me avoid missteps, but there are these awful times when he's busy and I'm still expected to go. I went solo to a very private New York screening of *The Crossing Guard*, followed by dinner. The director, Sean Penn, had invited only five guests, and I found myself plopped, terrified, between Bruce Springsteen and his wife and band mate, Patti Scialfa. Bruce and Patti were kind enough to keep things on my level by exchanging stories about our kids, which would have worked out okay except I simply could not cope having Sean, Tim Robbins, and Susan Sarandon seated directly across from us. The basic fact of my profound admiration for them left me tongue-tied and paralyzed.

The last time I went to the Emmys with David, he was nominated for Best Supporting Actor in *John Adams*, a show that really mopped up that year. I had promised myself I'd behave, but being introduced to the show's main actress, Laura Linney, proved to be too much. I was obsessed with her latest independent movie, *The Savages*, about a dysfunctional brother and sister (played with searing honesty by Philip Seymour Hoffman and Laura, respectively) trying to help their long-estranged father at the end of his life. I'd just barely recovered from shepherding my own mother through a major health crisis, and *The Savages* had been my lifeline. I'd been watching that movie over and over, almost compulsively, and I think I kind of frightened Laura Linney because I just could not leave the poor woman alone. All the *John Adams* people sort of moved around in a pack and it was pretty hectic, so I'm not sure she actually figured out who I was or why I was there, but I'm pretty sure she won't forget me. Everywhere Laura turned on her big night, there I was tugging at her elbow, desperate to share just one more episode of Mother Brigid's battle with her dastardly HMO.

Maybe the SBDs actually have our own interests at heart when they keep me from traveling. Sometimes I think it's best for David's future job prospects if I stay out of his business as much as possible. I've kind of come to welcome SBD interference if it means we'll be able to keep paying off the mortgage. But I simply must draw the line when whatever job he's doing involves contact with horses. *I'm* the horsey person in this marriage. I grew up riding—I *taught* David to ride. I thoroughly resented missing *Two Fisted Tales* (he was a ghost sheriff rolling into town on a dusty black horse, ready for a gunfight) and *Dreamer*, set in the Kentucky horseracing world. David was playing a wealthy, evil thoroughbred trainer, and he knew it was eating my insides to miss out on the fun. He'd call at night to tell me all about what a thrill it was to be near the racehorses—I'm still mad at the SBDs for keeping me away from those glorious creatures.

Mother Brigid does not believe in SBDs.

—God was looking after the children. They needed you at home.

—Ma. I willingly gave up my career for my children. I just wanted the freedom to pop down for a night and pet a real working racehorse for one second. Is that asking too much?

—Be careful what you wish for, Susie.

She may be right. Because now I think the SBDs have found a way inside my head. I am convinced they've opened a new department devoted exclusively to Influencing Susan's Selection of Disastrously Inappropriate Pets.

Did I mention that greyhounds don't fly?

Aircraft cargo can be left on the tarmac for hours these days—something about new security procedures following September

11, and the problem is these thin-skinned dogs cannot tolerate extended exposure to extreme temperatures. Who knew? Well, actually, *I* did; I *was* warned, but I was not in my right mind at the time, and told myself no problem was insurmountable. Now the implications are starting to sink in.

I'm still Lilly's main focus. She follows me everywhere I go, waiting till I settle so she can flop down on one of her various beds. She naps with her eyes open—it's a slightly creepy, glassy-eyed trance thing some greyhounds do. I can't get over how she manages to simultaneously be unconscious *and* maintain eye contact. Lost in thought at my writing desk, the room quiet, I'll glance over and there's Lilly in the corner, gazing at me.

They tell you not to choose a greyhound if you're looking for a watchdog. Lilly rarely barks when I'm with her, other than a polite little yip at the door when she wants to come inside after doing her business. I do believe she'll protect the house if she thinks it's called for—she busted right out of that half-asleep trance one afternoon in my office, charging straight at the window, startled by a roofer who was checking our gutters outside—but mostly she saves her vocalizations for when I'm not around.

When the family was here, all my outings had to be pre-planned and negotiated with the support crew. It was hard to leave anyone in charge, especially the men, because all hell would break loose—nonstop pacing, constant barking, and defecation. I've learned I can't possibly stick any house sitter who has a day job with an animal in this state, so Lilly will definitely be driving down to New Orleans with me, and I'm determined to try to improve things a little before we start the long trip south. Since David went down there earlier this month to start the season and find us a house, I've been conducting a series of experiments. There's a camera on a tripod in the family room. I turn it on just before I leave, and I now have endless videos of Lilly barking frantically, gnawing on the kitchen door, jumping up on the desk.

It's stress. The crate is useless—all that twaddle in dog-training books about how crates make dogs feel secure? Lilly despises the crate, and the minute I'm out of sight she loses all interest in rubber toys stuffed with tasty peanut butter.

I'm having flashbacks to infant feeding schedules. When I was nursing the boys and outings were timed to the last second, I kept naïvely reassuring myself that my parental responsibilities would simplify. Now I know better; if you're like me, you actually never stop planning your life around your children. I have zero regrets about giving up work to be with them at home, but after two decades it seems like I shouldn't still have to be negotiating with sitters every time I need to leave my house.

It's natural to feel suffocated by this situation. The irony is I also kind of like being stuck at home. I've always had reclusive tendencies, but I've never really had a way of indulging in them till this year. I've never lived alone. Now that the boys are gone, I miss everyone, but to be honest I'm enjoying this peaceful Lilly-imposed confinement far too much for it to be good for me.

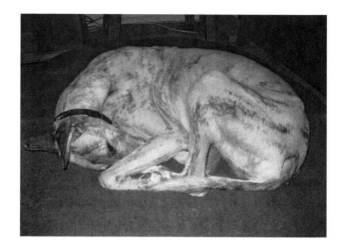

The rescue people say she needs company. Their theory is Lilly has been surrounded by other dogs her whole life, and a second greyhound could make her feel more secure. It's a little frightening how tempted I am to try this, but what if a second dog has even more complicated issues? I have to keep reminding myself of the original plan—my job right now is to ready things for our six-month southern relocation, and make sure the SBDs don't figure out a way to wreck it. I'm not supposed to suddenly switch course and open a convalescent home for traumatized dogs.

What makes things worse is that Lilly is still suspicious of David. *(The big one likes her too much. You want him to leave.)* He's really tried, but because he comes and goes so much it's hard for them to bond. In the months before he left for New Orleans, he hit on a sort of Pavlovian technique, banging her metal food bowl at mealtime:

David bangs the bottom of the metal food bowl. BONG BONG BONG BONG BONG.

DAVID. Lilly!

Lilly appears somewhere.

DAVID. Oh, there you are, you sweet thing. Has she forgotten about you, you poor dog? Come here. You're lucky someone still loves you.

David goes to a cabinet to look for the bag of dried dog food.

DAVID. Let's see what we have in here.

Lilly sidles around to look in the cabinet too. David finds the bag.

DAVID. Oh, look at that! You lucky, lucky girl. I wish I could have this. Let me just smell it.

David opens the bag and takes a ridiculously big sniff inside the bag.

DAVID. Mmmmmn . . . mmmmnnn . . . I can't believe you get to eat this food. I want this.

David scoops food from the bag, crashing it into the metal bowl making lots of noise.

DAVID. It's too bad she doesn't care about you anymore. Thank God for me. Okay, let's get your cheese.

David, at the refrigerator, looks for the Parmesan cheese in the bottom drawer. Lilly sidles over to look in the bottom drawer too.

DAVID. Oh, cheese, oh, cheese, oh, cheese, oh, cheese . . .

David finds it, sprinkles lots of cheese on the dried dog food.

DAVID. This is how you know I'm the one who really loves you. I'm not stingy like her. Let's have a listen.

David shakes the metal bowl with the dog food and Parmesan cheese. David and Lilly listen. Lilly's chin quivers.

DAVID. Oh, that sounds so good. I have to hear it again.

David shakes the bowl again. Lilly jumps to see in the bowl.

DAVID. Oh . . . oh . . . I have to taste it.

He puts his face in the bowl and pretends to eat.

DAVID. Aaarrgghh, aaargghh . . .

Lilly's chin nearly quivers off her head.

DAVID. Oh, I wish, I wish this was mine. See what I do for you. I don't even eat it all.

He puts the metal bowl on the floor in its elevated stand.

DAVID. There you go, you lovely girl. Don't you like me better than her? That mean, mean person?

Lilly eats ravenously, scattering dried food over the floor. David, for the time being, sadly believes they are now best friends.

Tragically, just when Lilly began to appreciate him somewhat, David had to leave again, and when he returned one weekend they were back to square one, Lilly slinking to a remote corner the minute he brought his suitcase through the door.

The whole situation doesn't sit right with me. David has made a lot of compromises for his family, passing on jobs that meant too much emotional upheaval for the kids. David loves the stage more than anything, but theater was particularly taxing for the little ones because plays run for months with only one day off a week. I've always feared he feels confined artistically by his family, and now that children aren't an issue I'm very glad he's got more options. The thing is, I've promised him we'll be together. We can't let a dog (particularly one that doesn't even seem to like him much) come between us, but still I feel a responsibility to Lilly. It's not her fault I didn't do my homework about common greyhound emotional quirks before taking her on, and it's not David's fault either. The fault is all mine.

We are not kennel people—Arrow almost died after two weeks at the best place we could find one summer. Since then, we've always managed to find house sitters for the pets, but Lilly's more of a challenge. We have a problem.

My mother was raised in the country. She considers herself the authority on animal-related matters, and firmly believes in a tough-love approach.

—Get rid of it.

—Ma!

—The dog is defective.

Ma made sure we had plenty of pets growing up—she saw animals as essential to our education as human beings. As with everything, she delivered strong opinions on how they should be handled. Many of her edicts made perfect sense: *Dogs need company and regular walks. If you can't commit to walking, don't get a dog. If you're not home during the day, get a cat.* Other rules were traumatizing: *Too many puppies in this litter? They'll kill their mother, and it's impractical to feed by hand. Drown the extras in a barrel.* (Colette, at age thirteen, was actually given this task. She still has nightmares.)

Ma was always disturbingly quick to cull the herd of any she deemed unfit, and as a result my siblings and I each carry grudges about particular favorites. We also feel some gratitude; Ma gave us ponies, and each of us had the chance to experience the birth of puppies and kittens at home. This was both thrilling and hair-raising. Too often she forgot to get the adoption process under way until after a litter's crucial neutering window had passed. Lacking appropriate partners when puberty struck, dog and cat siblings sought physical gratification with one another. More than once we were overrun with multigenerational, incestuously engineered canine or feline gangs.

Most of Ma's pet mismanagement happened during her Roman Catholic phase. I sometimes wonder if the pope had some influence. Avoiding birth control made sense, but how does pet euthanasia jibe with the pope's position on assisted suicide and the death penalty?

Ma insists religion had nothing to do with her negligence. She says she was pretty messed up in the head during those years for a multitude of reasons, and too distracted to pay much attention to animal management. Whatever the cause, witnessing the results of my mother's pet foibles up close was definitely a valuable education. Her practical rules about dog walking and such have stayed with me, always in the back of my mind, but her mistakes are with me too. It's as if our more unfortunate pets were siblings out of favor, and the helpless shame of not being able to intervene when a beloved family pet was not dealt with compassionately and responsibly still weighs heavily. I think this is probably one of the main reasons I feel a growing sense of anxiety about how to manage Lilly, and I've always made a point of being conscientious with family planning, both animal and human.

I'm in awe of parents we know who have teenagers and still manage to gracefully fold new babies into the household, intended or not. We discovered our limits when I had a pregnancy scare a few years ago during perimenopause—you'd think our world had come to an end. The doctor eventually explained it's not unusual to have false positives on home pregnancy tests when your hormones are going through the change. (Personally I think the SBDs were behind it. The Department of Birth Control Malfunctions, maybe? The closer we are to that golden time when spontaneous travel with David is finally possible, the more devious those nasty little buggers could get.)

There's one woman I know who took great lengths to have children late in life. Gina grew up in a large family, and wanted at least five kids of her own. Birth complications led to a hysterectomy after her second child was born. Having considerable financial means and a mutual taste for adventure, Gina and her husband decided to avail themselves of new technology: a program known as "in vitro fertilization and egg donation," in which the ovum from a "donor" is fertilized with sperm from the intended father and then implanted in a surrogate.

I cannot stress enough how hard it is for me to relate. An *accidental* pregnancy for someone my age I can sort of understand. But on *purpose*? I'm having enough trouble taking on a needy dog at this stage in my life. Gina and her husband are now overrun by toddlers. They'll be in their seventies when the last is still in college. Why do they seem so ecstatic?

NOVEMBER 25, 2010: THANKSGIVING DAY

Experienced empty-nester friends have warned that holidays will not be idyllic—I might not completely enjoy having everyone descend on my new peaceful, ordered life. *No way*, I thought. *I'll be over the moon when they come home.* As it turns out, the veterans are a little bit right. I'm glad to see everyone, and of course I wouldn't have it any other way, but to be honest I've kind of enjoyed my break from coordinating everyone's schedules and needs. I've taken so well to this six-week hiatus that a mass Thanksgiving invasion feels a little like—well, like an invasion. Everything's just so hectic all of a sudden.

Sam arrived last week (he has a beard!) followed by Eliza. A college-aged nephew flew in yesterday and David's mother is here too. Ben and David landed this morning, as did David's sister and her husband, all with different airport pickup times. Lilly does not recognize anybody and keeps hiding behind my legs *(They're very tall. They won't stop touching you)* and the dishwasher is threatening to die. Truly, I would not have it any other way. I am *very happy*, but I wish they'd all stop asking what time the next meal is.

Once everyone is sufficiently stuffed with turkey and pie and

Mother Brigid is snoring over her prayer book in the living room, I grab Lilly's leash so we can clear our heads for a second.

We've stepped up the walks lately, mostly on advice from a canine separation-anxiety specialist, Wendy. I showed Lilly's videos to Wendy and pointed out our chewed-up kitchen door, hopeful that this woman with a reputation for magically transforming troubled dogs would sort us out. Her solution? Plenty of exercise, supplemented by drugs. Apparently nothing else will work for a dog this age. Lilly's too set in her ways, and separation anxiety is practically guaranteed to escalate dangerously if you don't squelch it quickly. Dogs have been known to destroy everything handy when they're left home alone—they will chew up an entire sofa, eat into walls and insulation, even crash through a plate-glass window to get outside so they can track down missing owners.

The desk in the mudroom is right in front of a huge window. I am positive Lilly jumps up there when I'm gone because she wants to see outside better. What if she decides to smash through the window? I've heard of dogs dying that way. This is not just about keeping the dog from damaging the house; it's about keeping the house from damaging the dog.

I was horrified at the notion of zonking Lilly out, and it took quite a while for Wendy to convince me to try medication. I'm not a drug person, but given my anxiety on airplanes, I do understand that meds can be useful as long as they're not overused. We'd been trying holistic solutions, lunging at anything anybody suggested:

spiking her water dish with Rescue Remedy, spraying an atomizer of canine pheromones just before going out, even propping a large stuffed Toys"R"Us dog next to Lilly's favorite bed along with a pair of my dirty socks. Nothing was working. I kind of think that stuffed dog made Lilly even more freaked out than she already was. We're out of alternatives.

Once Wendy assured me we'd be using a very low dose and it could be stopped anytime, I decided it was worth a test run. Along with the medication and extra walks, Wendy says training exercises are a must. Like children, dogs need structure and a sense of purpose. I'm now armed with all kinds of fabulous treats. Freeze-dried liver and duck strips provide heaps more incentive than your average Milk Bone. It's kind of a game and amazing how much more willing Lilly is to process simple hand signals when you've got the right motivation. *(She holds her hand up and looks at you, and if you lie straight down, it's DELICIOUS.)*

As always, everything has to be slightly tailored greyhound-wise. I have to keep training sessions cheerful and short or Lilly will collapse under all the scrutiny—her clinginess sort of evaporates and she abandons me, scramming out of the room. I'm not sure if it's genetic or a result of the confined kennel lifestyle where certain skills were not a priority, but the greyhounds I know are not likely to "come" on command. They'll learn it, sort of, but not in any reliable way. Linda says on the rare occasions Dylan and King accidentally slip out the gate, calling them back is pointless. The best thing to do is simply run in the complete opposite direction, really fast, because they will chase her to see whatever exciting thing she's found. (This should work for Lilly. She won't let me out of her sight.)

I've embraced Wendy's reward-based training method, which is popular with many dog behaviorists these days. Like with kids, it's all about positive reinforcement: "capturing" the expected good behavior (almost like taking a photograph when Lilly does what you want) and instantly celebrating it with treats. This is much more fun than having to pounce on bad behavior. Most trainers agree that no matter what, a regular obedience routine will keep Lilly out of what Wendy calls the fight-or-flight "Lizard Brain" and put her more in the thinking "Wizard" mode, which helps keep her anxiety at bay. The drugs are only there to take the edge off.

It's been about two weeks since we started the Prozac and so far she's the same dog—still freaked out in the home-alone videos, unfortunately. Wendy tells me to give Lilly more time, and stick to that steady exercise regimen, which is not a bad thing. Our neighborhood is great for walking, and lately my favorite route has been around the corner to check on the chickens.

My friend Rose has a sort of urban farm situation: organic vegetables, honeybees, and about half a dozen hens scratching around in the shrubbery. They sleep in this fabulous fox-proof henhouse, cleverly designed with special doors above the nesting loft so you can easily reach in and scoop out eggs. Rose had to banish their rooster to the country because he was too obstreperous, crowing imperiously long before sunrise and bullying her dogs.

Without a rooster's active participation, the hens' eggs are no longer good for anything but breakfast. Rose's chickens don't seem to particularly mind missing out on the chance to reproduce, but Rose does—she'd been counting on a few chicks every now and then. So occasionally she orders pre-fertilized eggs online, pops them into a nest (she marks them first so she can tell them apart from the eggs her chickens lay themselves), and watches to see if any of the ladies will take to them.

Apparently not all hens feel the "broody" instinct to sit on eggs, so Rose keeps a few extras warm on her kitchen counter, in little electric egg-carton-type incubators with clear plastic lids so the family can watch them hatch up close. Next, the big challenge is to get a couple of the hens to accept them. Rose says it's a little nerve-wracking to open the henhouse trapdoor, choose a random nest, slip a handful of featherless, limp little foundlings in, and leave them there, fingers crossed, hoping they'll connect with a mother and survive the night.

I find the whole situation fascinating, and I'm kicking myself I didn't think of raising chicks when our kids were little. I may have been too preoccupied and controlling to risk taking on litters of kittens and puppies like my mother, but chicken breeding was so doable. This missed-opportunity sensation keeps coming up lately—I've been dwelling on imagined parenting mistakes: Sam would never have had his football injury if I'd followed my instincts and forbade the sport in the first place. Ben wanted to switch schools in sixth grade, and then changed his mind. I'll always wonder what it would have been like for him if we'd made that happen, and what about Eliza—was she really asleep under all that earthquake rubble or did she wake up before David got to her? It's alarming to think we've done all we can for our children and now they're almost on their own; I keep wanting to turn back the clock for a do-over so we can make things a little more perfect.

Rose's hens don't really like us. Lilly's chin is quivering—it's a thing she does when there's something potentially tasty nearby, like cheese, or, apparently, chickens. *(They stretch their necks at you and say* Praaaawk. Puk-puk-pukaaawk. *You could catch them, but you don't think she wants you to.)* Good thing we use a leash, because the ladies are out on their own today, hunting bugs in the bushes. No chicks—it's off-season. On the way home we pick up the pace a little; I'd love to sneak upstairs for a quick lie-down before it's time to think about dinner. I'm really not used to all this activity. I must be getting old—my knees don't seem happy.

After a nap, I'm still pretty stiff, and it's worse the next morning: Ma's eighty-ninth birthday. We take everyone out for lunch (a relief; no dishes) and present Ma with the dream gift she's been hinting about all year—an iPad. She's still yearning to be connected with the priests and out-of-town family by e-mail, and she has a hunch she'll be able to manage this thing better than the computer we tried years ago. By the time I go over iPad basics, drive her home, and carry all the birthday loot up to her apartment, my knees are not cooperating. They don't seem to want to bend. It's getting harder and harder to pick up my feet—I have to slide along in an awkward sort of shuffle. Tomorrow I may have to ask the kids to walk Lilly, which won't work out very well—they tend to give up when she freezes, paws clamped to the pavement halfway up the block.

I think I need a doctor. This is not like me.

Why do mysterious, worrisome health mysteries always seem to happen at the end of the business day on a Friday?

Actually, why do I even bother to ask that question? It's so obvious. Score one for the SB frigging Ds.

10.

Anatidaephobia

Anatidaephobia:
The fear that somewhere, somehow,
a duck is watching you.
—Gary Larson

An early memory:

I am three years old, perched, with my mother, high on the bank of the Wissahickon on a hot summer day. We are watching people feed ducks in the water below us, and I'm hoping there are no worms in the moist earth under my fanny. My dress is very short and we don't have a picnic blanket.

Just as I take the first bite of a slightly soggy bologna sandwich, a disturbance erupts down on the opposite side of the creek: an agitated duck. Could be my imagination, but the duck seems to be coming toward us, and the duck is pissed, thundering relentlessly across the creek, quack-

ing incessantly, louder and louder. When the creature hits land below, the three-year-old me sees it as enormous. I look anxiously to Ma for direction, expecting at any moment we'll be gathering milk cartons and napkins to make a dash for it.

I recall this vividly. Just as the duck's physical mass is distorted in the context of my own size, the speed at which it advances up the bank, in my memory, is perceived in cinematic terms—like a chase scene in one of those creature movies from the '50s where the camera cuts back and forth between a lumbering giant spider and its prey. You're sure the panicked heroine will be able to outrun the beast if she can just stop screaming and get a move on. In my memory Ma and I are suspended, watching in bewilderment as this monster duck beats a path in our direction, neck stretched, wings flapping. In the seconds before contact I think, *It's a white duck—white ducks don't bite, right?* Then *OUCH!*—the savage creature's beak connects with my tender, exposed haunch.

My innocence was lost that day, along with my bologna sandwich, which, apparently, is what the duck was after. Ever since, I've been particularly cautious around waterfowl, making tonight a challenge: Eliza and I are watching *Black Swan.*

David is an Academy voter, and every fall the studios mail him DVDs of current Oscar contenders. They are supposed to be strictly for his consumption, but given I'm not in any shape to go out to the movies I feel no guilt screening this one before he comes home for Christmas. There has been zero improvement on the knee front—the doctor at the emergency room was stumped, along with my GP. They've tested me for the scary stuff and can find no sign of anything wrong, which does not necessarily mean much, according to Colette, who is my go-to person whenever there's a health mystery afoot.

Colette reads medical journals for kicks. She keeps a whole collection of reference material on a shelf in her kitchen, where ordinary people store their cookbooks. She has her reasons. Colette's been suffering for decades from an evolving assortment of suspicious ailments, some quite debilitating. Now semiretired (partly because she's not strong enough to work as hard as she once did) she's determined to get to the bottom of things, steadily becoming an expert at navigating the British National Health System, which is no small achievement. Colette is five years older than I am, and with her health complications, she has the edge when it comes to understanding what can happen to women of our certain age. If she has no direct experience with a given problem, there's always someone in her circle who does. (Her mother-in-law; her hairdresser; her husband, Badger; a neighbor's cat.)

When Ma went through her recent two-year health crisis, Colette was an excellent resource; even if she doesn't know something, she'll research like a pro. No matter what disease I toss at her, Colette can be counted on to become an armchair Dr. House overnight, launching into a long-winded analysis of the situation. Sometimes I lose the thread when she's on a roll, partly because there's too much to take in, and partly out of sheer terror.

—*Autoimmune conditions run in our family, Sizzle.*

—*What's an autoimmune condition?*

—*Remember Ma's thyroid and Cousin Buckety's diabetes? I'm still feeling my way here, but it's mwah bwah bmah buddly fuddle FIBROMYALGIA splunk. And sometimes it's POLYNEUROPATHY gabba gabba MULTIPLE SCLEROSIS jinglehopper bindy darp, because it could be POLYMYALGIA RHEUMATICA or MYALGIC ENCEPHALOMYELITIS or simply ADULT ONSET DIABETES gumble stumpy-bump.*

—*Wait, what did you say? Is that serious?*

—*Never mind, Sizzle. I'm sure it's nothing. Just remember to tell the doctor you are HYPERMOBILE, and you had ERITHROBLASTOSIS when you were an infant, and blap smap MIGHT END UP IN A WHEELCHAIR spap girrap.*

—*Slow down a second, I'm looking for a pen—ow.*

The knee thing has spread to one wrist. Trapped on the sofa that first week, feeling completely unproductive, I decided to redo our Rolodex so our house sitter, Gaillard, can easily find plumbers and whatnot while I'm in New Orleans. That job ended up taking a couple of hours, and next morning, after easing myself gingerly out of bed and creaking downstairs to the kitchen for breakfast, one painful step at a time, the simple act of using my writing hand to lift a container of milk from the fridge made me scream.

I'm beginning to understand this is definitely not an ordinary injury. This thing is colonizing itself, attacking any other part of my body that's under the slightest strain. I'm praying it's temporary, but I have a horrible feeling I'm dealing with something serious and degenerative. It started so abruptly, it keeps getting worse, and the doctors are ominously quiet. Colette says it can take years of testing to identify and effectively treat some of the more complex autoimmune conditions like rheumatoid arthritis and lupus. People get gradually worse and worse, waiting for answers, and often a diagnosis does lead to wheelchairs and skilled nursing rather than a satisfactory cure.

I am not going to think about wheelchairs. . . .

A lot of friends are telling me it could be Lyme disease, even though I have no recollection of ticks on my body, ever, and two blood tests have come up negative for Lyme. I got a call the other day from the daughter-in-law of a friend of Ma's, a middle-aged woman in Maryland named Margot. Margot has been through a long ordeal with what she believes is a low-lying, chronic form of the disease.

——*You have to find the right doctor. I went undiagnosed for three years until I found a specialist who did a different kind of test and put me on IV antibiotics. I'd send you to my person but I think she lost her license. Just get your hands on doxycycline.*

——*Thanks, but my doctor says I should wait——*

——*Well, he's wrong! You can't wait! It goes to your brain next! I started losing my mind; I was getting lost going home from the market. Tell your GP to give you doxycycline, and if you feel better after three days I guarantee that's what's wrong with you.*

It's bad enough having to hobble around like the thousand-year-old man, calculating every move I make so as not to waste what little energy I can muster, my trip to New Orleans next month hanging in the balance. Losing my marbles would be the last straw; I kind of need them this year. My first book has recently found a publisher and the editing phase will be starting shortly. This is the one positive thing I'm holding on to—my body may be going rapidly down the tubes, but the novelty of professional purpose is helping fend off despair, like a gift.

Am I losing my marbles? Either this Margot person is my salvation or a crackpot. Maybe she's both. Either way, what's to lose? A few days ago I called up Dr. Maxwell's office and wheedled enough doxycycline out of him for a week.

Maybe *Black Swan* will distract me.

All we know is it's Natalie Portman playing a young ballerina who goes crazy under pressure when she's cast as the lead in *Swan Lake*. I love that ballet—I saw Nureyev play the prince at Lincoln Center as a teenager and never got over it. *Swan Lake* is a classic, about an innocent, virginal girl enchanted by an evil sorcerer. Odette is a swan by day and a girl by night, and the only way the spell can be broken is if some man declares his undying love to her. The catch is the man has to remain faithful. If he cheats, she'll be a swan forever.

One evening, a prince out hunting by the lake spots Odette and invites her to a ball. But the evil sorcerer sends his witchy daughter Odile in disguise instead, dressed just like Odette but in black. (The same dancer plays both parts. Odile is the real challenge. There's this killer "Coda" during her big seduction of the prince, where Odile has to do thirty-two consecutive fouettés—turns *en pointe* with a whiplash kick in between. Not many ballerinas can handle the Coda.) Things end badly when the prince swears undying love to the imposter Odile, and Odette decides to drown herself in the lake.

I read an interview with Darren Aronofsky, the director of the movie. Apparently *Black Swan* is a kind of werewolf story, except instead of a wolf-man, Natalie Portman's ballerina is a modern-day swan-girl. This sounds perfect for a girls' night with Eliza—I love a good dance movie, and a creepy one like this should be a welcome diversion.

Famous last words.

Lilly settles into her bed in a corner of the TV room, keeping a wary eye out for Joey. He's figured out he's stuck with her, and I think he's decided to attempt a sort of truce/friendship by testing Lilly's boundaries, always creeping in to settle near where she's resting.

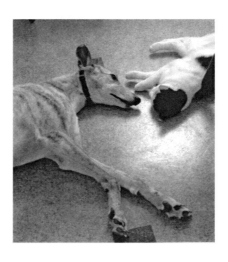

The deeper we go into this movie the more vulnerable I feel—
it's like the director is out to get me, hitting all my tender spots.
There's a ton of mother-daughter stuff: Portman's mother is played

by Barbara Hershey, a wonderful actress we don't get to see much of now that she's older. She's playing Erica, who, like me, gave up her own career (dance, in this case) to raise a child. Now Erica's the stage mother from hell. All these festering self-doubts about my own parenting mistakes come roaring to the surface—how is Eliza taking this? I know I wasn't as awful as Barbara Hershey, but still, the whole setup is getting under my skin.

And the body horror! At first it's subtle (close-ups on Nina's feet, flexing till they crackle before she gets out of bed in the morning) but it's so close to home—every morning since my symptoms began I lie in bed, testing each joint gingerly before I pull myself upright and gimp awkwardly into the bathroom. Portman's Nina (a painfully shy, stunted twentysomething woman-child with a bedroom full of pink satin teddy bears and ballerina music boxes) has a lot of trouble convincing her director that she can handle the seductress Black Swan part. One night Nina pushes herself so hard working on the thirty-two fouettés she collapses on the floor. When she peels off the toe shoe, her big toenail is practically coming off, oozing blood.

Things go from bad to worse. Nina becomes increasingly alarmed, noticing strange bloody scratches right in the area where a wing might connect with her shoulder blade, and the skin around the scratches is all bumpy, like a plucked chicken. Plus, there's this whole self-mutilation angle. When Erica sees her daughter's scratches she says, *You're doing it again*, and clips Nina's nails, accidentally-on-purpose cutting some skin with these badass nail scissors, making her yelp. After Nina snags the prized part in *Swan Lake*, the company's former prima ballerina, Beth (Winona Ryder, quite striking as the bitter has-been), jumps in front of a car and winds up in the hospital. Of course Nina has to go visit, and sees horrifying jagged infected stitches and nasty pins sticking out of Beth's leg up close with this God-awful *Psycho*-esque music screeching.

As we press on, Nina is clearly unraveling, pushed to the breaking point by all the pressure. She's bulimic, naturally, and she keeps hallucinating, seeing her own threatening doppelgänger from the corner of her eye (evil Nina, dressed in black instead of pink, lurking in mirrors). Her paranoia really kicks in when the company is joined by Mila Kunis as bad-girl ballerina Lily (properly spelled in the credits!) and the director points out Lily could play the Black Swan with both wings tied behind her back. (Lily literally has huge black wings tattooed on her shoulder blades.)

I can't help connecting this to myself. My body is haywire. Is it real, or is it all in my mind—menopausal hysteria?

Nina hallucinates a hot lesbian sex scene with Lily (guaranteeing tremendous box office draw, if you ask me) made particularly freaky because when Lily goes down on Nina, her face morphs into Nina's, and she says, *My sweet girl,* which is what Barbara Hershey always calls her daughter (good heavens, I can't even look at Eliza) and then tries to smother her with a pillow.

One thing I'm noticing, lying here on the sofa: my knees. Is it possible I can bend them a wee bit more easily than I could when the movie began? Is the doxycycline kicking in? I've been on it for four days, and Margot said this was a test: if I feel any improvement after a few days there's a good chance I do have Lyme disease. Holy crap! Now what?

Another thing: this movie is fascinating. The dancing is electric, the women are acting their tights off, and the director has us on the edges of our seats. There are all these intriguing details. The entire story is told from Nina's unreliable perspective, and there are millions of interpretations you could make a case for: Nina's schizophrenic, and her mother doesn't exist. Or actually her mother does exist, but she's been secretly molesting Nina. Okay—maybe Nina's mother exists, but Lily doesn't. Or, Lily exists but she's nice, not threatening. Nope—nobody exists in this movie except for Nina, who is not a dancer at all, she just wishes she was; she's one of those haunting people you see pinballing down New York's sidewalks talking to themselves. We may never find out the truth, and that's totally fine, because it's a Rorschach inkblot: what's perceived reveals as much about the viewer's own subconscious as anything else, and besides, the whole thing is riveting no matter what.

For me, the penny drops the night before Nina's first performance, when she flies home in a panic and slams the bedroom door on her mother. Tiny black feathers are popping out of her gooseflesh and THEN, she takes a step, and her frigging knees snap backward, like a duck's legs. It's so extreme it borders on ridiculous, but the essence hits me right in my solar plexus: Nina's body is staging a mutiny against everything she's striving for. This

I understand in my very soul. Here I am, on the brink of a whole new season of undisturbed marital bliss, my children are launched, and there's this unexpected gift of a beginning: a book being published. Like Nina, everything's going my way, but what happens? A complete physical collapse happens, that's what.

I shout to Eliza *THAT'S ME!*

Lilly startles awake from her bed in the corner and bolts from the room, and Eliza looks at me like—*WTF, Mama? You're turning into a swan?*

11.

Fossils and Quacks

JANUARY 2011

I've stumbled on a war.

After reading and talking and surfing, here's my unscientific take: there are a lot of people out there all hot and bothered about ticks.

There are roughly two camps, and they seem to hate each other intensely. One camp tells us Lyme disease is rarely contracted, easily detected, and quickly treated. This is the camp that tested me twice, didn't find anything, and is unimpressed when I tell them my knees have not always looked like giant raspberries. This camp seems interested only in one measly ankle, which hurts less than anything else but apparently looked a little funny on an X-ray. They're waiting for results from an ankle MRI, but mostly I get the impression this camp thinks things would be much easier on everyone if I'd just take some Advil and buzz off. Oh, to buzz off and get on with my life . . . I used to be able to lift my feet off the floor. I participated in a triathlon last summer—I did not always shuffle around like a geriatric version of Frankenstein's monster— I'm kind of frightened by how little the first camp has to offer.

Then there's the second camp. The doctors in this group say Lyme and other tick-related infections are extremely sneaky and persistent, with many different symptoms, and they believe traditional lab tests are unreliable. This camp likes to put people on risky long-term courses of antibiotics. I'm not big on antibiotics, so I'm not ready to fully commit to this camp quite yet. I'm also not big on dementia, total incapacitation, and death, which, according to the second camp, can happen if you have Lyme disease and you don't get rid of it.

The first camp thinks the second camp are unscientific quacks. The second camp thinks the first are antiquated fossils, and everyone's hurling accusations about mistreating patients for devious financial motivation. Quacks say fossils are on the take, profiting from the continued use of outdated tests they originally helped develop, and amassing oodles of grants and lecture fees based on their mainstream pedigrees. Fossils say quacks make a killing on the dangerous IVs they hook patients up to for months, even years, at thousands of dollars a pop.

It's not only patients who are upset by all this discord. Fossils don't like to do interviews because of a barrage of vitriol and death threats from patients and advocates in the quack community. Quacks don't mention their specialty on websites, because powerful fossil supporters are hell-bent on putting them out of practice. Caught in the middle are a *ton* of frantic sick people (me included), venting on the Internet, grasping at straws. And there are plenty of straws out there, including alternative healers even most quacks and fossils scoff at—fringe-type practitioners with herbs, minerals, diets, and eccentric tests.

Here's my status update: I'm still stuck in Philly seeing doctors and continuing the doxycycline. Aches persist, radiating out into many more random joints. After a routine dental hygiene appointment, for example, my jaw doesn't want to open all the way anymore. I'm constantly monitoring myself for cognitive impairment, but if I am impaired, how will I know? How does a crazy person identify their craziness? I'm aware my symptoms could be a sign of all sorts of things besides ticks. But the word on the street is if you have a tick infection and it goes untreated too long, it can invade your brain, and then you're cooked. I am not going to discount tick involvement until I've looked under every rock.

Appointments are exhausting. Every outing has to be carefully calculated with meticulous consideration of parking lot layouts and such. A simple trip to the grocery store is a major expedition, and meals are reduced to anything with minimal prep, like soup. As much as possible, I'm inert, which would be perfect for Lilly if it weren't so hard for her to relax when the cat's around. *(When does that rabbit sleep? It's everywhere.)*

I haven't given up on dog training. It's not easy, because I'm always forgetting to keep treats close at hand for rewarding good behavior. Wendy wants Lilly to get used to the clicker instead of constant treats anyway—this is a little metal thing that makes a "click" noise. You're supposed to just click and give her a treat so she can associate the sound with positive reinforcement. But Lilly's too jumpy. She definitely loves the new treats—as soon as I open the cupboard where we keep her freeze-dried liver and duck strips, her chin starts vibrating with anticipation—but I must be doing something wrong with the clicker, because she floors it out of the room every time I pick the thing up. *(It's nasty. It tells you something bad's going to happen.)*

Lilly's chin quivers for more than just treats now. I've found her erogenous zones. We have these long, blissed-out sessions; she's discovered she loves being stroked along her brow and in the tender crevices in front of her ears. If I stop, she's never pushy asking for more. She sort of pauses for a second or two, waiting to see what will happen, and then gently shifts position, inviting more attention in the most subtle, respectful way, almost forgiving me in advance in case I've had enough: a slight lift of the chin, or a single paw gesturing discreetly, like a blessing. I can tell she's dying for more; her chin betrays her. I can't help wondering if anyone ever had the time or inclination to stroke this lovely sensitive animal during her working years.

Always in the back of my mind is the looming possibility that I may not be able to justify keeping a complicated dog if my health doesn't improve. I want so much for this to be Lilly's Forever Home. One foot in front of the other.

Another thing Wendy stresses: If a dog has any kind of separation issues, it's vital to make departures and arrivals as boring as possible. I sort of knew this; our first dog, a sweet Australian shepherd mix named Aya, used to get so excited when we came home she'd lose control and pee all over the place. We were using a training guide written by the Monks of New Skete, who explained that we could avoid messes by not talking to Aya till she'd been outside. The technique worked, although it took a while to get our friend Tom to cooperate. Tom, an actor, was kind enough to stay at our house sometimes when we traveled. But he liked doing things his way, and he loved how special Aya made him feel when he came home from auditions. Tom sincerely appreciated Aya's attention, insisting it was worth the mess—until the night he brought home a lady friend.

This was one of those romantic third-date's-the-charm-type

situations, and Tom was optimistic. Everything had been carefully planned: jacket and tie, reservation at a romantic high-end restaurant, a bottle of good wine stashed in the fridge for later, and clean sheets on our guest bed. Tom had been counting on Aya's usual rapturous welcome routine to provide any needed character references and help seal the deal with his extremely attractive date—the theory being any guy who is loved this much by a dog has got to be worth putting out for.

When Tom and his lady arrived at our house after dinner, Aya put on a show. Egged on by Tom's cries *(Aya! I'm home!)* she felt moved to express her delight with even greater abandon than usual, whimpering in ecstasy, rolling over on her back to expose her belly. And when Tom finally bent down to tickle her, Aya released the waterworks with gusto, her thrashing tail serving as a sort of irrigation device (like a long-range sprinkler on a golf course) thoroughly drenching everything within five feet (Tom's coat and tie, the date's pretty dress), directing most of its force with remarkable precision straight into Tom's appalled open mouth *(Aya, stop it—glug—augggh, no!)*.

You'd have thought the spark of romance would have been extinguished, but apparently this particular lady friend was a sport. If it hadn't been for Aya, Tom and his dream date would never have ended up in our shower. . . .

After time spent with Tom, it could take a week or so of the silent treatment to settle Aya back into continence. Lilly is a tougher nut to crack.

Right now the objective is to keep her out of that "Lizard Brain" mode altogether so her destructive impulses won't be triggered. I try to time my doctor visits for when helpers are available: our housekeeper, Lillian, or our friend Gaillard, who rents an apartment above our garage. Whenever I return, Lilly gets the prescribed cold shoulder, kind of like my old Robot Mama routine at Eliza's school drop-offs.

I'm becoming more and more aware of possible parallels between my concerns about this animal and my protective attitude while raising our children. You know how when things get sort of dicey, and you can't shake the feeling there's some lesson you're supposed to be absorbing? A building sense of doom, as if everything's only going to become worse until you surrender to whatever it is? There's something about my growth as a human at stake here, maybe something I didn't quite resolve while raising children. I can't put my finger on it yet, and I am beginning to wonder how the joint business factors in. Why is this happening right when I can finally travel with my husband?

Nothing to do but press on. Lillian, Gaillard, and the O'Briens have also taken over the dog-walking regimen, which is a huge help, and fortunately Wendy pays house calls. I'm doing everything I can think of to untangle the worst of my medical puzzle and get Lilly shipshape so we can both head to New Orleans as soon as possible.

Fossils don't have much to offer. Two highly regarded specialists have made it clear fourteen days of doxycycline is plenty. Only a fool would want more, and if I insist on being a fool, I'll have to go elsewhere, meaning, I guess, to a quack. They have no other ideas.

I do think the doxycycline has been helping a little; it's subtle, but I'd like to take Margot's advice and continue. I'm on the lookout for nasty side effects—none so far. I have only a few weeks' worth of the stuff, and a doctor's blessing is required. I feel sort of like an addict trying to plan the source of my next fix, and while I plan, I'm dabbling in the fringe because it seems best to use an open-minded, multipronged approach. First things first: Mother Brigid's holy cotton balls.

These are Ma's latest Answer To Everything: A while back, a couple of the icons at her church unexpectedly started oozing this myrrh-type substance—literally, fragrant oil squished out of the hands and eyes of the saints in the pictures for a couple of weeks. The priests were low-key about it. The Orthodox take on weeping icons is they're a sign of pending sinful-type trouble in the world—either that or the devil is messing with their heads. I personally have no opinion either way, and I'm flat-out desperate anyway, so when Ma suggested I try rubbing the stuff all over my joints, I figured I had nothing to lose.

On her return from church, Ma presented me with a Ziploc baggie containing a couple of little oil-soaked cotton balls. The oil is colorless, and the scent, although faint, was immediately noticeable when I opened it. A lot of my affected joints are extremely tender to the touch—my knees and wrist feel like fresh bruises—so I was a little tentative rubbing the cotton balls over everything. While I waited for signs of change, I kept thinking, *If this works, does it mean I have to convert?*

Not an altogether unpleasant experience, but so far holy cotton balls are about as curative as Advil (meaning *not*). What's most important is that Mother Brigid is satisfied she's done her bit. On to the next.

There's a handful of alternative people I trust, decent healers who've successfully cured an assortment of our family's afflictions when the medical community was stumped. My favorite is Siegfried, a homeopath in L.A. I've consulted with Siegfried for decades—he's a whiz at treating children's mysterious coughs and stomachaches right over the phone, but I know from long experience Siegfried can be a little grouchy if I argue in favor of certain immunizations, or decide to opt for antibiotics instead of following his directions. I highly doubt Siegfried will endorse my doxycycline habit any more than the fossils have. I know him too well—Siegfried's going to tell me it's all about caffeine, sugar, and dairy products. As much as I adore him, I have a hard time believing I can fix myself by simply cutting out Godiva chocolates on Valentine's Day. I'm not feeling up to another confrontation just yet. I'll save Siegfried for later.

Our local acupuncturist, Bella, has actually detected traces of Lyme disease in my system. She suspects the carpet cleaners I brought in after David left used something toxic that may have sickened me enough to allow lurking Lyme bacteria in my system to attack and cause my symptoms. I guess anything is possible. . . .

I keep going over stories of fellow sufferers—it's amazing how many women my age develop joint trouble. I have a feeling doctors don't find middle-aged women all that interesting. We complain too much; we're not worth bothering with unless we've got something more life-threatening and sexy, like breast cancer. Maybe we need to start rattling the cages, marching (shuffling) on the White House. The AIDS community did it in the '80s and '90s; now it's our turn. If this is not ticks, what the heck is it?! ABBA Ladies Unite!

It turns out Lilly's trainer has been down this road as well. Wendy seems like a bright woman. After overhearing me vent on the phone one day, she offered her story. A few years ago Wendy began to feel kind of achy and tired. One day she had an initial consultation for a dog with a perfectly ordinary behavior problem. She says she'd usually be able to discuss a dog like this quite easily, but at the new client's house, Wendy's mind went suddenly blank and she could barely string two words together. The problems didn't go away, and after much trial and error, Wendy got help from a tick rheumatologist in New Jersey, one of the top doctors in the Lyme-literate community (in other words, a quack).

Wendy's big on research, and she is good at putting things in layman's terms. Apparently the fossils rely on tests that were developed back in the 1980s, when Lyme was just beginning to be studied. There are new blood tests available now, which can detect minuscule traces of the elusive bacteria. Wendy says these newer tests are being used routinely on animals when Lyme is suspected.

But for unexplained reasons (like what? Lack of reliable double-blind studies, or something more shady and financial?) they have not yet become a mainstream tool for diagnosing humans. In other words, if I were a dog, or a cow, I'd have a much better chance of finding out what's wrong with me.

Wendy's doctor found a tick disease and put her on long-term antibiotics. She's got her marbles back now, and she is urging me to drive two hours to New Jersey for tests. Having done plenty of legwork, Wendy thinks the Lyme-literate doctors in our immediate area are not up to snuff. Apparently there are some *real* quacks out there, but Wendy's rheumatologist seems to stick to the rules, such as they are.

—Drive two *hours*? I'm not sure I can do that by myself. Did you?

—I had no choice.

—How long did it take you to get better?

—Years.

—*Years*? God. I have to travel. And this dog—two hours round-trip plus an appointment is too much time alone for Lilly. Oh my gosh, what am I going to do?

Wendy gives me a long look, and waits.

—That was a hypothetical question, Wendy.

—Okay.

She waits.

—Why, what are you not saying?

Wendy sighs.

—Look, Susan, you've done a lot for Lilly—she's adjusting

nicely, but you are in an extremely difficult situation. Even if you had your health, taking dogs with separation issues on trips is not a great idea. Every new environment will trigger her fears. I would not blame you if you decided to find a new home for Lilly, and if you do, you can feel good that you've given her a great start.

I've been waiting for Wendy to bring this up. Driving her to it, daring her, dreading it.

I look at Lilly, dreaming at my feet. The sight of her always soothes, mysteriously, the way transcendent art can heal the soul. A meditation. Articulated muscles and streamlined tendons; a perfect instrument, ideal in proportion, almost vibrating the potential for power and speed but also heart-meltingly, exquisitely fragile—a long-limbed, brindled Stradivarius violin, silent but ready, sprawled decorously on my oriental carpet, one ear cocked in my direction.

It's the visual that drew me to greyhounds in the first place. Now this reserved, majestic creature is my friend. She's counting on me.

—I don't think I can. I mean—this is my dog. If change is too disruptive for Lilly, how's she going to deal with a new owner?

—Well, it's just something to consider. You don't have to decide right now. Maybe you'll get better faster than I did.

It seems to me there are two clear options.

One: give the situation a little more time.

Two: fire Wendy, put Lilly in the back of the car, drive downtown to the Ben Franklin Bridge, get Lilly out of the car, and jump, together, immediately, into the icy, roiling Delaware River.

So.

Probably first I should try the quack camp.

The O'Briens agree to take Lilly for the day, so that's something. Praying she won't cry the whole time I'm gone, I make the two-hour drive to a leafy colonial suburb in New Jersey. I park close to the entrance, figuring if I'm too stiff to get out of the car, at least I can call from my cell phone for assistance.

Thankfully assistance is not necessary. Instead, I hobble in to have my blood drawn by Dr. A, who looks, surprisingly, more like a neighborhood soccer mom than an evil, devious IV-pushing quack. She gives me a rundown on how Lyme-literate doctors diagnose and treat a tick disease, tests my range of motion, nods soberly, and offers me enough doxycycline to last till the labs come back. Phew!

Dylan, King, and Lilly

Lilly's playdate, as I'd hoped, has gone smashingly. She's not all that enthusiastic meeting boisterous dogs, but with other greyhounds it's different. I'm not sure exactly why this is. The books will tell you greyhounds are sort of socially picky, preferring each other's company. It may be because all their early life is spent in a sort of exclusive pack, and a Labrador or Scotty seems alien. Whatever the reason, Lilly's like a different creature around Dylan and King, despite their vigorous male energy, and when I take her home she whines the whole way.

The first time Dylan and King came to our place for a visit, Lilly was thrilled. Everyone was, actually, except Joey, who I had forgotten to put away. The O'Briens don't have cats, and King immediately got some exercise streaking after Joey up two flights of steps to the third floor. Fortunately Joey managed to make it inside the box springs of the guest bed in the nick of time, and interestingly, our winding third-floor stairs didn't faze King in the slightest on the way up. Linda says King's not known for his brains (there is some suspicion that he was not much of a success on the track; in fact, his trainer may not have even bothered to try him in a single race). This was proven when he galloped madly up without much thought (*That's a rabbit! Get the rabbit!*), but then seemed to go completely blank on the reverse, stiffening at the treacherously narrow top step.

Lilly is still cautious with our stairs. She has this long warm-up ritual when it's time to go up for bed—there's a lot of yoga stretching (downward-facing dog)—and if I forget the hall light, she'll wait, panting up at me from the bottom of the unlit stairs. When I turn it on, she still has to pace back and forth several times, sort of revving the engine, before trotting daintily up.

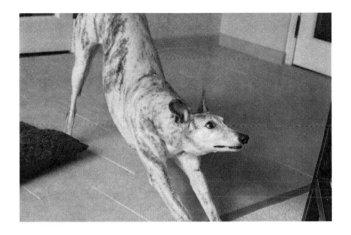

I can relate. I rely completely on banisters now. If I suddenly realize I've left something downstairs while we're on our way to bed, I can't just turn around midflight and go back, because Lilly will want to do the same, and she is guaranteed to lose her footing on the steps mid-turn and might actually tumble all the way back down. (This has happened.) Instead, I continue climbing, to the top, pointlessly wasting energy, cursing my forgetfulness, and wait for Lilly to reorient herself so I can lead her back down again.

Anyway, Lilly can't get enough of those O'Brien boys. Her tail goes up the minute they're around, her ears tip forward; she's literally smiling. Arrangements are made for them to take her off my hands for a couple of weeks while I fly down to New Orleans and wait for the quack's test results. The O'Briens are a godsend—the drive I planned is out of the question for now, given the circumstances, and it's high time I joined my husband.

NEW ORLEANS, FEBRUARY 2011

Dirty little secret: I was nervous about New Orleans. After all my fantasies of happily-ever-after on location, the truth is I had no idea if this new life would be as wonderful as I'd hoped. I have work to do, and what about this health thing—will I be a burden to David while he's filming *Tremé*? At face value, the reasons for my delay coming down here were innocent, but in a sense I was sort of relieved. Maybe all these years he's *liked* being off on his own. Why would he want to suddenly have to live with some whiny, disabled woman who's totally preoccupied with her crazy dog, a dog who doesn't even like him? How's it going to go? It's bizarre to feel like a guest in my own husband's house.

I can't help wondering if frequent separations are the key to our success—no risk of overfamiliarity. Maybe I really have been wrong about the SBDs all this time—were they actually on our side, keeping us interested in each other by never quite giving us enough time together? I know the SBDs are a fantasy, but the subconscious is a powerful thing. Did I subconsciously *choose* a dog who would keep me out of David's hair? What about those theories about illness, that it can be created out of fear? Did I *make* myself semi-disabled so as to avoid inflicting my Lucy Ricardo alter ego on my husband?

But from the moment I spotted David smiling at the airport last night, I could tell we'd be fine. There were flowers waiting on the kitchen counter, dinner by candlelight, a comfortable sofa, and my favorite breakfast provisions. The house is in a quiet neighborhood, not too far from some pretty good shopping, with a yard for Lilly (so much for *that* plan). The only disappointment: the altitude on the flight did a number on me——I really thought the doxycycline might be helping, but after the trip down here I'm fully back to square one.

David doesn't have a printer, and I need one for all sorts of reasons, so on our first morning, we head out for errands and a tour. I'm trying to figure out why everything feels so familiar. The only other time I've been to this town was last year when we brought the boys down for a couple of nights over spring break while David was filming a few episodes of the show's first season. Now, I'm beginning to understand what the fuss is all about. There's nothing like New Orleans——it's almost like visiting another country. But why do I feel as if I'm home?

David's a great guide. Because of my immobility we've done most of our viewing from the car, and managed to cover quite a lot, despite the fact that anywhere you go here, you are likely to be delayed. The roads are gas eaters. There are all these one-way streets with wide median strips, and every destination requires negotiating a series of elaborate doglegs and U-turns. Plus, there's always a parade going on somewhere in New Orleans, and where there's a parade, everything stops. Nothing to do but wait and enjoy the scenery. There's plenty to see——I can't get over the live oaks, strung with years of Mardi Gras beads, their long limbs arching across all the streets. I think the cemeteries fascinate me most of all. This city is built on a swamp, so everyone has to be buried aboveground in elaborate stone crypts and mausoleums. New Orleans is all about show; this is where you should live if you haven't outgrown the childish urge to dress up. Not just for Mardi Gras. Masquerade is like a religion—deadly serious—there are endless excuses to put on costumes, and the favorite trends seem to be Indians, Baby Dolls, and Skeletons.

We drive through the Lower Ninth Ward, past empty lots and houses with somber post-Katrina body-count symbols painted on doors and boarded-up windows. We park close to the levee so I can drag myself up the iron staircase to see where it broke. I've been trying to understand and prepare for this, reading Tom Piazza's excellent novel *City of Refuge*, about two families torn apart by the disaster. It's staggering to think of the water, all over these streets, well above our heads. People drowning right inside their homes.

You can hardly go anywhere without catching a glimpse of the Superdome. My own troubles are sliding slowly but surely into perspective.

Here's an important tip: It's good to keep your car windows rolled up on Bourbon Street. I know it rains a lot certain times of the year here, but not enough to sanitize the party district in the French Quarter. New Orleans is one of those places where you can walk outside with a drink in your hand, and Bourbon Street smells like a great big frat house at the peak of rush: decades of vomit embedded in every nook and cranny. If you dug a sample out of just one crack in the sidewalk on Bourbon Street and tested it, I bet you'd score a DNA medley of the Southern literati elite—just think of all those tortured wild boys who ruined their livers here: Faulkner, Capote, Williams . . . It's amazing they got any writing done in this town.

We find a printer easily at the OfficeMax in a shopping district near our house, and stop at the mall on the way home. This is where a déjà-vu sensation begins to overpower me.

David has a date with a Genius at the Apple store. He also needs a special pillow from Bed, Bath & Beyond, which is off-limits for him because of their pumped-in air freshener. So he drops me off to find the pillow and meet him at Apple when I'm finished.

Malls are pretty much the same everywhere, but that's not what this feeling is about. This feeling goes back decades, to when nobody had heard of OfficeMax, and the Apple store was just a twinkle in Steve Jobs's eye. It goes all the way back to our first months in Los Angeles, sometime in the early 1980s, when I could walk like a normal person, and David could use a public restroom without a handkerchief clamped over his face because of the toxic cleaning fluids. When we floated everywhere in a haze of early love.

We had moved to a completely new city for a TV series then, as now, and we had only one car. Even the dullest errands were fun because we were usually together. With the arrival of children, time became a valuable commodity. Now, partly because of Lilly's separation issues and partly out of habit, we still take solo turns for Philadelphia shopping runs—so I literally can't remember the last time I spent an ordinary day like this out in the world with my husband. Laboring across this Louisiana mall, the weightless sensation I felt as a blissed-out new bride some thirty years ago floods back incongruously. I'm struck with awe at our good fortune. After all these years, even if I'm falling apart at the seams, I still feel a catch in my throat when I spot my man bending over the latest gadget in an Apple store.

Tremé is an ensemble show, which means David only works two or three days most weeks. He did have to go in early this morning, though, and after breakfast I putter around acquainting myself with the kitchen, then settle on the sofa to do a little thinking. Amazing: nothing on my mind but my own work for a change. Children squared away, dog temporarily stashed, mother in another state entirely. Toward the end of the business day, just as my body is telling me I've done enough laps between the kitchen and the living room for tea and so forth, and it's time to turn off the brain and pass out in front of Wolf Blitzer's news hour on CNN, my cell phone rings.

It's an urgent request from Ben in Texas. He skipped the dorm lottery because he wants to move into an apartment with some friends next year. They've already missed out on one place they found because they didn't move fast enough. He needs me to print his e-mailed application, cosign, and fax it to the new prospective landlord immediately so he and his roommates can snag this other place—if Ben loses it he's basically homeless next year.

This is not the kind of job you want to do when your cognitive abilities are on self-imposed investigation due to mysterious tick-related possibilities. Glad we opted for a printer with fax at OfficeMax yesterday. David set this thing up last night at his desk in the living room and it prints great. Checking my e-mail, there are a couple of dire-sounding ones from the O'Briens. Apparently Dylan and King got overexcited and went after each other this afternoon. There was damage done in the form of ripped throats *(ripped throats?!)* and a frantic dash to the emergency clinic. King, identified as the instigator, is on probation now, wearing a muzzle.

King

Good grief. I call Linda. She says Lilly was in a completely different room when things went down; this was just between the boys. The miracle is the O'Briens had to leave Lilly home alone when they rushed the boys off to the vet for stitches, and when they returned a few hours later, she was asleep. No crazy leaping through windows, not even the slightest trace of doorknob chewing. What's that about?

Linda seems calm about the situation, but I can't help assuming Lilly's future welcome at the O'Brien household is kind of in the balance. Now what will we do? Our housesitting tenant Gaillard is great about pitching in, but he has a day job, and Lilly's not safe home alone yet. I can't stand the idea of a kennel. Greyhounds don't fly, and that drive, with or without a dog, is still out of the question for me.

Wendy is right. Everything points to the fact that I've been impractical adopting a delicate new animal right when it's time to start traveling, and I feel like a jerk for causing this impossible situation. If I try to rehome Lilly, the rescue association will insist on taking her back into their system, and I don't know if I can stand it if she ends up in greyhound limbo. (Eliza's Child Protective Services episode all over again! Or like Ben, under a bridge, if I don't fax this stuff in time!) Linda says retired greyhounds are much harder to place these days, given the economy. Practicalities aside, I've fallen in love with Lilly, and when I think of her with some other person, it breaks my heart. To be honest, I'm jealous. She's *mine*!

This can't be about my needs. What's important is this gentle dog has probably never had a real relationship with a human before. Lilly has earned her Forever Home, and she's offered the gift of her love and trust to me, of all people. I don't want to let her down.

Am I truly going to have to decide between a life with my husband and a commitment to a dog? And if so, what exactly does it say about me that I think there's a choice? I really am an idiot.

I print Ben's forms and fill them all out, checking and rechecking for mistakes, make a note of the landlord's fax number, and, just to play it safe, keep the printer instructions on hand when I settle down at David's desk to perform this fax operation. It's extremely important I type in the number correctly. The lease application asks for our bank accounts and social security numbers, and you definitely don't want to fax private information to the wrong person.

Hm. There's that déjà-vu sensation again. What is it this time? Back in the 1980s in L.A., faxing was not even something you could do. Never mind.

I've learned (given current handicaps) to assemble all necessary materials before beginning a job like this. There is some urgency because business hours are almost over, but I carefully take my time gathering everything I can think of next to the printer before settling in. (Fax number? *Check.* Reading glasses? *Got 'em.* Printer instruction manual? *Right here.* Application all filled out? *Yup.*)

My cell phone starts ringing in the kitchen—oh no, is it about the dogs again? Whatever it is, I'm not going back there. They'll have to wait till I'm sure I've got this exactly right.

Okay. Put the form in the tray and type in the fax number. Check it to be sure it's correct. Check it one more time. Yes. Time to hit Fax. Here we go!

A little round thing lights up in the window on the machine. It spins promisingly. Waiting, waiting.

Still waiting. Still spinning. What's going on? Why is it not faxing?

I ransack "Frequently Asked Questions" in the manual, trying not to lose hope. It's beginning to dawn on me what my déjà vu is about this time: that frigging Ivy U Common Application! Come on, people, let's get this over with so Wolf Blitzer and I can take our nap!

FAQs say, *If you can't fax, first check all your connections.*

Okay. I look behind the printer.

Power: connected, obviously, or the machine would not light up.

USB to computer: not necessary at the moment, but yes, there is one of course. I just printed the forms.

Phone cord—*oops.* No phone cord? Didn't the printer come with one? *Fine,* I'll steal the one from the phone in the kitchen. Where *is* the living-room phone jack? It must be around here somewhere. . . .

Unbendable knees do not lend themselves to looking under a desk in an unfamiliar house to see if your husband has connected everything thoroughly. (I challenge anyone over fifty to get down on the floor while maneuvering completely straight legs—just try it. Picture a giraffe confronting a half-empty watering hole.)

Finally I'm lying on my back, most of me under the desk, legs flailing feebly, like an upturned beetle (please, my reading glasses—where are they? I can't see a thing) and this, of course, is when my cell phone rings again, all the way back in the kitchen; I'll never get there in time. Hopefully it's not Linda about the dogs, or Ben with some new urgent housing-related need. Most likely it's Ma, either forgetting I'm not home or wondering if I got here all right. I don't want to talk to my mother right now, not with this Lilly problem in the forefront. If she worms the Lilly business out of me, one thing will lead to another, and I'll be hurling accusations about puppies in barrels. Let it ring, for both our sakes.

After a brief flirtation with despair (upon discovery that there is actually no phone jack *at all* under this desk—David is just not the faxing type, I guess) somehow, miraculously, I find my second wind. Like a marathon runner at the twenty-mile mark when single-minded determination replaces lactic-acid burn and exhaustion, I rip the printer from its moorings and lurch across the room with it (David would have a conniption if he knew what I was doing) to the only phone jack to be found in this hell-hole, which of course is down near my ankles and there is no elevated surface whatsoever handy. I dump the thing on the floor, do my giraffe/beetle routine again (ow, ow, ow—*NO*, where's that fax number?! Oh. Found it. Never mind) and plug the thing in. It is 5:54 p.m. in Texas when, finally, Ben's application is on its way. Now I can die.

It is true what they say: The nest may look empty, but it is not. Not till the fat lady sings. Or something like that.

When David comes home from work, Wolf Blitzer is blasting. I'm lying flat on the living-room floor next to the printer with my legs sticking straight in the air, determinedly reflecting on all there is to be grateful for: Our children are thriving. The O'Briens are in love with Lilly. (Linda's vet thinks the dogfight had something to do with their catching the scent of a whelping fox in the woods by their house, and things will settle down once the season's over.) David has a job. We are together. All is well.

Next morning it occurs to me I never got around to checking those cell-phone messages from yesterday. Turns out it wasn't Ben, Linda, or even my mother—both calls were about test results.

Dr. A has come up trumps: according to her special quack-type tests, I do have something, but it's not Lyme. It's called anaplasmosis, a tick-related coinfection usually found in dogs, not humans. (Somehow that figures.) The symptoms seem to match too (joint pain, muscle aches, confusion). The best news is that of all the tick problems I could possibly have, this one's the least dangerous cognitively, and the simplest to fix. The treatment actually is what I've been taking: oral doxycycline. My various fossils insisted that any quack I went to would try to trick me into one of those costly/risky IV situations for months. It's encouraging Dr. A is not even mentioning that route, but still, she wants me to continue the oral doxycycline for a total of four months before having another blood test.

While I'm digesting this information, I follow up on the second message, from the fossil that ordered the MRI. According to this highly respected doctor, my only problem is I have tendonitis in one ankle. (That's *it*?) I do remember twisting an ankle walking Lilly last fall, but when I bring up the quack's anaplasmosis diagnosis, the fossil gets kind of huffy on the phone. It's up to me if I want to be stupid when all I really need to do is take Advil (*again* with the Advil!) and rest the ankle (which, *duh*, will not be a problem given the incapacitating knee trouble I am supposedly imagining).

So: Here I am, right in the middle of a war zone. I'm the last person to take chemicals if they're not really needed. We all know how antibiotic overuse can turn your system into a hive of drug-resistant bacteria. But still, it would be so nice to get back to normal and this may be my only chance.

It's time to consult with Siegfried, our homeopath in L.A. If anyone can talk me off this ledge, Siegfried can. Siegfried knows me, we have history, and at the very least he will be comforting to talk to. He'll definitely understand that this is more than a twisted ankle, that it's not normal for me. But most important, Siegfried hates antibiotics like the plague—I don't think he's ever really forgiven me for ignoring his advice one time when Sam had strep throat and Siegfried wanted him to cut out ice cream and treat it with herbs. If he has a better idea than Advil or four months of controversial chemical ingestion, I'll try it.

It takes a while to get through to Siegfried because of the West Coast time difference. Just hearing his familiar voice on the line gives me a tiny taste of what it might feel like, having a helicopter's rope ladder drop to the rooftop of your storm-flooded Gulf Coast house. I gulp out my story.

—I know what you're going to say, Siegfried. Yes, I was probably drinking too much coffee and I do love chocolate. But this is serious. I have no idea if I should trust this doctor, and I'm in a real situation here, so please don't yell at me—

—Take the doxycycline.

—Say *what*??

—I've seen this up close, Susan. Antibiotics are the only solution available. Tick infections are real, underdiagnosed, and devastating. Keep in touch with the mainstream doctors if they want to look for something else, but do not even consider letting a possible tick disease go untreated.

—Wow. I was totally not expecting you to say that. Are you *positive*? Because this other doctor told me all I have to do is rest and—

—SUSAN.

—Yes?

—Take. The. Drugs.

Well I guess that's that. When a holistic purist like Siegfried says take the chemicals, the battle's over. Score one for the quacks.

12.

Coincidence?

I'm on a genealogy binge. Everyone's home this summer, and for some reason I feel an urgent need to acknowledge our shared roots before the children run off again.

—Kids.

—Yes?

—Your ancestors had slaves.

—SLAVES?

Each night at dinner I update them on the fruits of my research. They're only half listening—this stuff bored me, too, when I was their age, and I used to tune out whenever my mother brought it up. Maybe interest in family history is a developmental thing, something you can't access until you pass your own half-century mark.

Hoping to keep our kids' attention, I focus on dirty family laundry.

—The Draytons came here from England via Barbados in 1678. They settled in South Carolina, and established two plantations—

—With *slaves*?

—Yes, sorry to say. But our Philadelphia branch redeemed itself by moving north before the Civil War. Two Drayton brothers, Percival and Thomas, actually fought directly against each other, on opposite sides of a big battle. How's *that* for family dysfunction?

My mother's mother, long deceased, produced two batches of children divided between different marriages, and there are caches of family memorabilia scattered all over the globe. One cousin, Nina (the eldest of my generation and a product of our grandmother's first marriage), shares my newfound drive to keep old stories alive. She and her husband, John, are putting together a web archive, and they've requested any interesting specifics concerning the family of our grandmother's second husband, my grandfather, Harry Coleman Drayton.

I've been putting this project off all year because I haven't felt up to rooting around in our cellar. There's a trunk down there somewhere, full of old leather-bound albums—family photographs dating back to the Civil War era. Nina and John have been patiently waiting for me to sort my body out so I can get down to it. I think the health scare and months of confinement have acted as a sort of catalyst, sparking my need to pass on history to future generations before it's too late.

Good news: I am myself again.

I took my doxycycline religiously, and spent most of the four-month course bouncing back and forth between sofas here in Philadelphia (Lilly snoozing happily by my side) and, when I could manage it, down in New Orleans. The O'Briens kindly offered Lilly an open invitation, which allowed me to admit that it's best not to rock her boat with a disruptive trip. I was happy to be free of that worry, but sad, missing her. Our rental's little backyard is so perfect for a dog, chosen just for Lilly, and it sits barren, like an unused nursery.

When a second blood test finally cleared me of the tick coinfection, I couldn't understand why I was as lame as ever. Dr. A's response was unsettling:

—*That's normal.*

—*Normal? When will I be able to walk?*

—*Give yourself time. Doxycycline can cause inflammation. That's probably what you're feeling.*

—*Wait. This drug is supposed to cure my tick disease, the symptoms of which are inflamed joints. You're saying the doxycycline has been actually increasing my pain?*

—*Give it time. Come back and have your blood drawn again in a few months. Try walking a little, see if you loosen up.*

Easy for her to say. Siegfried didn't have much more to offer, and, at a loss, it suddenly occurred to me I might as well work on that one ankle I'd twisted walking Lilly last fall, back before this whole thing started. The fossil who found the tendonitis told me to stay off the ankle until it was better (which, obviously, I had been doing) but it never occurred to me to try a treatment Eliza had success with back in high school. After missing two sports seasons due to Achilles tendonitis, physical therapy wasn't helping, and Eliza needed to play tennis in the fall. When we stumbled on something called Integrative Manual Therapy, the results were staggering.

Figuring I'd better address my ankle before embarking on a walking regimen, off I went to the local IMT center. At the first intake, Ginger the IMT lady (a fully licensed physical therapist) observed my general condition and offered to try working her magic on all of my joints, not just the twisted ankle.

——*You think you can fix the rest of me too?*

——*Might as well try!*

Why not? I thought.

IMT sessions are so pleasant you almost feel as if you're being duped. All they do is place their hands on you and breathe. I lay there, chatting with Ginger, playing with my iPhone, reading, napping, whatever, wondering why on earth any insurance company would actually pay for this. I didn't feel any better when I got off the table at the end of my four-hour treatment, but to be polite I scheduled another, figuring I'd cancel later.

Next morning I lingered in bed for a while as usual, gathering my courage for that first awful trip to the bathroom. (Mornings were the worst. The whole process of getting myself upright was tedious and excruciating: Roll over on least-painful shoulder—*ouch*. Slowly tuck arm under rib cage so I can use best elbow instead of impossibly dysfunctional wrist to push myself into sitting position—*ouch, ouch*. Haul feet over side of bed, gasping, put on ankle-support strap, and then, leaning heavily on bedside table because knees are not strong enough to straighten on their own—*ouch, ouch, ouch*—use bad wrist to haul myself erect because there's no other option, and finally, stand for a while recovering, breathing.) It would take about ten minutes to go thirty feet, Lilly hovering, stretching, and yawning, waiting politely for her breakfast and a pee.

The morning after that first IMT appointment, I braced myself for the agonizing roll out of bed. Was it my imagination? The shoulder seemed a little better. Did the arm bend a bit more easily? And the elbow—there was *no pain whatsoever* in the elbow for the first time in six months! The wrist was still kind of sore when I leaned on it, but the knees, the knees actually almost worked! It was stunning.

Waiting for my next session, I regressed a bit. But each morning after a treatment things would again dramatically improve, until one glorious day I leapt out of bed like a normal person and burst into tears. It's been over a month now. Aside from one toe that's still a little funky, I'm out of the woods.

I don't know if I'll ever be sure what was wrong, or what fixed me. But I do know this: If the slightest whisper of joint pain returns, I'll let the tick lady test my blood again at some point, but I will go to IMT immediately. To all interested parties seeking a local practitioner: Google *Integrative Manual Therapy Connecticut* to pull up the website for their headquarters. Best of luck.

The boys came home from college last month just around the time Eliza graduated and David finished the second season of *Tremé*. (They plan their schedule around the heat of summer and hurricane season, so he'll be on hiatus till mid-October.) As before, Lilly shunned each male arrival, skulking around, emphatically dodging all attention. David is philosophical about being treated like an intruder in his own home, and has applied himself to re-seducing her. He was feeling generally good about his progress until Linda O'Brien's husband, Richard, stopped by to pick up David and the boys for an adventure at his trapshooting club the other day. When I opened the kitchen door, Lilly jumped to her feet, racing past my crestfallen husband to greet Richard like a long-lost brother, completely confounding our theory that all men have to work for her trust. Richard tells us Lilly likes him so much because he's been feeding her when she's over there, which does not make David feel any better, given all his *Bong-bong-bong* dinner-bowl maneuvers.

I still carefully plan my outings with military precision, trying to avoid leaving Lilly home alone, ever, but at least now that I can walk again I'm feeling more hopeful we'll be able to keep her. She continues to trail me everywhere, flopping onto the floor strategically so she can keep me in her sight line. Even when it seems like she's dozing, the kids tell me Lilly's ears swivel back and forth, bat-style, rotating motion detectors tracking my movements around the room.

We may never understand why Lilly prefers me to the Morse men. David thinks there must be a tall, mean male kennel hand in her background. A rescue dog of any kind is an enigma, and with a racing greyhound you have the added mystery of the past career. The identification tattoos inside Lilly's ears both fascinate and upset me, a disturbing reminder that Lilly was nothing but an exploitable commodity in the world she comes from. A number. Like the sudden urge to retrieve our abandoned family history, I wish Lilly could tell me her story—how she lost the tip of that ear on the right, and what the cruel-looking scar on her front leg is about. If I knew more about where she really came from it would be so much easier to figure her out.

But despite unsolved mysteries, little by little this dog is coming out of her shell, revealing herself on her own terms. Our neighborhood greyhound group arranged a really fun play date at a canine agility-training space last February for a half dozen locals who'd been cooped up all winter. Lilly was in top form, just like all the other dogs, and it became clearer than ever how they thrive when surrounded by their kind; parading gaily around the arena like a gaggle of preteen girls cut loose at the mall, tails thrashing, leaning into one another shoulder to shoulder and hip to hip—a twenty-four-legged amoeba automatically switching directions on some undetectable inner groupthink cue. I have to press for more of these get-togethers.

And I can't get enough of Lilly's glorious thirty-second speed demonstrations. I have to catch her in the right mood, usually sometime in the late afternoon when she rouses from her nap and starts hinting about dinner. We have a pretty decent-sized lawn out back, and if I take Lilly out there and dance around a little (I can dance now!), she gets this goofy grin on her face, spinning madly in place for a while sort of winding herself up, and then she's off for a few gleeful laps around the yard, just for the joy of it. I've learned to stay very still when Lilly's on a tear, because she loves to dash straight at me and veer off at the last second. Lilly knows exactly where she's going, and if I mess her up by trying to step out of the way, she's likely to knock me right over. Eliza's been trying to capture her on camera—not easy to do.

We hardly worry at all about Joey anymore. Lilly has no interest. Even if she did, this cat takes care of himself.

It's such a relief to be able to go down the cellar stairs so easily now. In the trunk, I've unearthed US Adm. Percival Drayton's

Civil War belt buckle and red tasseled sash, and I've found photographs of him and his brother, Thomas, online. Percival, commander of Union warship USS *Pocahontas*, spent a rather stressful afternoon shooting directly *at* his Confederate brother, Gen. Thomas Drayton, who was holed up on shore at Hilton Head. There's a picture on the Internet of a dazed crowd of Thomas's former slaves flanked by a few Union soldiers the day they were officially freed.

Both brothers survived the war, not on very good terms, understandably, but they did have a reconciliation of sorts toward the end. Thomas, being on the losing side, fell on hard times and became quite sickly in his final years. Percival never married, but on his deathbed he bequeathed a decent sum of money to his destitute brother down south. Blood runs thick.

From the Department of Mysterious Coincidences: Percival and Thomas's father, William Drayton, served four terms in Congress. There's a glamorous portrait of William hanging in the White House, painted by none other than Samuel F. B. Morse, the Morse code guy, who David's mother is pretty sure is some kind of ancestor on David's father's side. Kind of fun thinking of our children's two distinguished forefathers together. Wonder what they talked about? No way to know. Too many questions and not enough answers. Like contemplating Lilly's mystery scars, all I can do is piece together scraps of evidence and guess.

I'm trying to be systematic, but it's hard not to go off on tangents. Everything's sort of mishmashed in the trunk, souvenirs from my mother's forebears nestled in the dark against a smaller collection of memorabilia from my father's side. My father's father's people, the Polish von Moschziskers, came to the United States much later than the rest of the family. The von Moschziskers were prone to estrangement according to Ma, and large branches of the family have completely lost touch. This is extremely frustrating because it seems like anyone from our branch who could really answer the questions I keep coming up with is no longer living. I'm deep in von Moschzisker territory, following a particularly intriguing thread, when the phone rings—my brother Felix.

Felix recently moved into his new dream house in Vermont, built from scratch, perched on a hill with a view of the Mad River Valley, and a few days ago we flew Ma up to celebrate his birthday. She hasn't traveled far since she became seriously elderly, aside from the odd overnight to services in Carlisle. The priests usually fix her up with a female companion while she's there, but on this trip to Vermont we winged it because Ma's in incredible shape right now—she hasn't missed her confiscated scooter for a second. In fact, when the nurse recently offered to return it, Ma gave it away to a fellow inmate.

Knowing this burst of mobility can lead to recklessness and accidents, I'm on guard. Felix, fifteen years my senior and a long-time bachelor, is not the ideal caregiver. He and Ma have had some epic clashes over the years, but they were both highly motivated to make her summer visit a good one. The older Ma gets, the more aware we become of the preciousness of time.

—Fe! How's the visit going?

—Great. Just exactly long enough. I'm about to take her to the airport now, and Suse, guess what she forgot to bring?

—Oh no. What?

—She ran out of colostomy bags this morning. Do you know where I can get—wait a second, she's yammering at me, I'm going out in the driveway. Be quiet, Ma, I'm talking to Suse.

(Clump clump clump.)

—Felix.

—Yes?

—Can I talk to Ma?

—Oh. Well, now I have to go all the way back in the house.

(Clump clump clump.)

—Susie.

—Ma?

—Susie, this is ridiculous. I don't need more bags, I'll be fine till I get home. I only told him that because I wanted his sympathy.

—Are you all right?

—Yes, I think we're both a little tired.

—Okay, Ma, I'll see you at home. Can I talk to Felix again? Wait—no, I have a question first.

—Yes?

—Why did nobody tell me Daddy was sort of Jewish?

—*What?* Your father was *not* Jewish. His parents were Sweden-borgian, which is unfortunate enough.

—But I'm looking at a file Colette sent me with some letters this woman in England wrote to Aunt Bert because they had the same last name. She sent Aunt Bert a photograph. They looked just like each other, and they both had little black poodles! She said she escaped Nazi-occupied Vienna just after Kristallnacht, and all her family died in concentration camps, and an American friend saw Bert's name in the paper, and the name von Moschzisker is very unusual, so—

—Oh yes.

—So you *knew* this? Why didn't anyone tell *me*? Was it a cover-up?

—No. We just couldn't prove anything, so there was no point in talking about it.

—Do *you* think Daddy was Jewish?

—Well, I always thought his father's nose was suspiciously large.

—Ma!

—I have to pass you to Felix now. He's standing here grumbling. Felix you're very impatient.

If we do have Jewish blood, it's sort of moot since we're talking about the patrilineal line, but personally, I'll take whatever claim to Jewishness I can get. I can't figure out if Aunt Bert ever managed to meet this one lone survivor face-to-face, but I certainly hope so, and I'm a little pissed at the von Moschziskers for being so tight-lipped. The news makes me even more determined to figure them out. Clearly, there's a big iceberg down there.

My father's grandfather, Franz Adolph Moschzisker, was a doctor, a scholar, and a commissioned soldier in the Austrian Army. He sided with the Hungarians in the buildup to one of their various uprisings, was taken prisoner, escaped, and fled to England, where he married an Englishwoman, Laura St. John. They had a couple of daughters, and for some unknown reason, Franz Adolph left them all behind, inexplicably added the prefix "von" to his name (as if it weren't long enough!), and sailed to America just before the Civil War.

When I finally understand what happened next, I can hardly contain myself till dinner.

My father believed his grandfather Franz Adolph's first English wife, Laura, died long before he married his second, my American great-grandmother Clara Harrison, in 1857. But another cousin has been investigating, and documents prove Franz Adolph's first wife, Laura, was actually still alive and kicking years after her husband "married" Clara Harrison (no certificate to be found) in the United States and had another batch of children, including the one with the nose: my grandfather Robert.

—Kids.

—*What?*

—We are Jewish, and illegitimate.

—*What* are you talking about?

David hasn't quite caught my genealogy fever, but not to be outdone by my colorful lineage, he reminds us of a tasty item on his own family tree:

—Kids.

—Yes, Papa?

—You have an ancestor on my side named Preserved Fish.

We have no background on Mr. Fish; he's just an item on David's tree, and I haven't been able to get my hands on David's family records yet. According to *Wikipedia*, Preserved Fish was a New York City shipping merchant in the early nineteenth century, and his first name, Preserved, had more to do with being preserved from sin than what one might imagine.

Colette cautions me to consider the context before judging Franz Adolph as a deadbeat. Back in the early nineteenth century, divorce was not available to any but the upper crust, and some people who went to the New World from Europe took the opportunity to reinvent themselves. And as for the Jewishness: upper-class Philadelphians in my grandparents' generation were a haughty bunch. They tended to intermarry and did not take much interest in outsiders. I imagine this cover-up, if it indeed took place, was a matter of simple practicality.

Still, it would have been nice if someone had prepared us a little, provided some kind of explanation. Did they really think we'd never find out? Maybe they didn't care. That hurts my feelings.

Despite not coming from the "right sort of people," Franz Adolph's son, Robert von Moschzisker (my father's father), did well for himself, especially if you consider his circumstances. Both Robert's parents (Franz Adolph and his second wife, Clara) died when he was still a teenager. I wonder if that's why we have all these unanswered questions. Was my grandfather orphaned before he was old enough to understand? Robert, who was no slouch, worked his way up from being a twelve-year-old law-office gofer to becoming Chief Justice of the Pennsylvania Supreme Court. He married well also: to Anne, the daughter of another self-made man, of Scottish descent, George A. Macbeth.

—Kids.

—*What*, Mama?

—You have a great-great-great and so forth grandfather who *may* have assassinated the king of Scots.

Sadly, we can't prove for sure whether Robert's wife, Anne, was related to that murderous fellow in Shakespeare's Scottish play. But what has always interested me is another coincidence: Anne's mother was also a Scot, a Duff, as in *MacDuff*, sworn enemy of Macbeth. This means when my father's grandparents married, two families with a serious history of differences became one. Talk about healing your family tree.

Nina and John have no idea what kind of monster they've roused—the more I've explored things both from the trunk and on the Internet, the more obsessed I've become. The genealogy websites are addictive—you sign up, plug in your own family tree, and then you can dig up more information when your people's names connect you with other trees. Mormons created these sites, I hear. Because their religion is relatively young, Mormons feel an apparent need to identify their lineage, the object being to gather the family in heaven by posthumously baptizing all ancestors who died before Joseph Smith came along and invented the one true church. (It's best not to get Mother Brigid started on this topic.)

I could lose myself forever on these websites, and I'm beginning to realize we have a real boomer phenomenon with this genealogy business. There are a lot of us middle-aged amateur detectives out there, contemplating our mortality, seizing this new tool to understand where we come from so we can leave a record. So our children aren't left, like us, with a trunk in the cellar full of question marks.

I almost lost track of Nina's original mission: to get a better handle on those slaver Draytons on my mother's side who came over from England. There are theories that Draytons descend from a hero of the Norman Conquest, one Aubrey de Vere. After distinguishing himself at the Battle of Hastings in 1066, Aubrey was awarded land by William the Conqueror, on which his children's children's children built a family home in Northampton that still stands—a rather enormous fourteenth-century manor, Drayton House.

There's a famous medieval artifact, the *Bayeux Tapestry*, which depicts the story leading up to and including the Battle of Hastings. Greyhounds are all over the place on it. And, another coincidence: Aubrey de Vere founded Colne Priory in Essex, where all the fancy de Vere earls are buried. When his wife, Beatrice, died, Aubrey became a Benedictine monk.

—Kids.

—Now what?

—Mother Brigid's not the only clergy in the family.

Aubrey was Benedictine, meaning *not* Orthodox, therefore not Mother Brigid's type. Mother Brigid's a purist. Orthodox Christians date back to the early followers of Christ, pre-schism, way before there was any such thing as a Roman Catholic. As far as they are concerned, the pope is marginal. But Aubrey and the *Bayeux Tapestry* do get me wondering: Could *Draytons* have had *greyhounds?* In Cynthia Branigan's greyhound history, she claims we have Celtic monks in particular to thank for the preservation of the greyhound breed in Europe during the Middle Ages. While everyone was busy starving and fighting wars and burning up art, the monks focused on what they felt was important, holed up in their sanctuaries, busily copying over the books of the New Testament and, yes, protecting greyhounds from extinction, as the theory goes.

Lilly has her own British roots. It's actually easier to verify her origins than those of the Draytons. The racing community keeps meticulous records, and it's believed all greyhounds in America can be traced back to King Cob, a gorgeous nineteenth-century British champion who was the first public stud. Lots of intriguing monikers in Lilly's tree (Big Whizzer! Wigwam Wag! The Firth of Forth! Stumps!), including her parents: Lady Godiva and Dodgem By Design. Lilly's father, Dodgem, had a pretty distinguished sire line, which includes King Cob and the legendary Downing: a red brindle Secretariat-type machine dubbed the Greyhound of the Decade back in the '70s. Downing was such a phenomenon that they profiled him in *Sports Illustrated*; he raced all over the country and became the first greyhound to ever be syndicated, eventually retiring to chase ducks around his owner's farm and reproduce, rather prolifically.

While on the subject of monks and dogs, I can't help dusting off the old dog-training guide we used for our very first dog— the one by the Monks of New Skete. Back when we first followed the monks' tips with Aya, I wasn't particularly hip to the nuances of monkness. Now I'm delighted to discover that the New Skete monks, who I assumed all along were Catholic, are actually Orthodox. Another coincidence!

—Of course they're Orthodox, Susie.

—Why do you say that, Ma?

—Catholics are too focused on the rest of the world to think about dogs. For the Orthodox, fellowship with nature, especially animals, brings us closer to God.

I'm not sure I really want to know what the Orthodox position is on puppies and barrels. . . .

The Book of Kells is one of the most famous monk-produced manuscripts. Interestingly, there are pictures of greyhound-type dogs all through it. Though named for the Abbey of Kells in Ireland, many historians believe the first edition of the manuscript was created in the ninth century by Celtic monks on Iona, one of the islands of the Hebrides off the western coast of Scotland. These monks eventually fled Viking raiders to Ireland, but despite all kinds of upheaval Iona was an important spiritual center for much of the Middle Ages. Many Scot kings are buried there, including our Macbeth, who was a real historical figure in the eleventh century.

Scottish history is fabulously juicy: Mary Queen of Scots sent to the block, bloody Macbeth, and Braveheart—not sure if that guy actually painted his face Mel-Gibson blue for battle, but he was definitely real: William Wallace, a hero of the fourteenth-century Scottish rebellion, hanged, eviscerated, and chopped to pieces by his British captors.

There's a great anecdote in Branigan's *The Reign of the Greyhound* about a contemporary of Braveheart, Elizabeth de Burgh, a fourteenth-century queen of Scots. Elizabeth's husband, Robert the Bruce, led the Scottish rebellion against England after Braveheart's bloody demise, and during the long struggle, Elizabeth was captured and held for years by Edward I, the British king.

The capture was sort of awkward because Edward I was good friends with Elizabeth's father. Due to the greyhounds' value as hunting dogs, they belonged exclusively to nobles at the time, with laws against commoners owning them. Elizabeth must have been a greyhound lover, and Edward I must have known this, because during her eight-year confinement, he instructed Elizabeth's captors to give her three greyhounds for company. Locked up together for eight years! Those dogs must have been thrilled. Makes my many months incarcerated on the sofa with Lilly seem like a picnic.

Of course I have to spend the next hour investigating Elizabeth de Burgh to see if this greyhound story is legitimate, and I'll be darned if I don't stumble on another coincidence.

As it turns out, Elizabeth was definitely lucky. There was another woman on the lam with her, a Scottish patriot named Isabella MacDuff, who, for all we know, may have been yet another ancestor, given that Duff is my great-grandmother's maiden name. MacDuffs back then were charged with the privilege of endorsing Scottish kings—meaning the only way to become a legitimate king of Scots was to have a MacDuff physically place the crown upon your head. But, when Elizabeth's husband, Robert the Bruce, claimed the throne, the cowardly MacDuffs were mostly siding with the British—all except Isabella.

There probably wouldn't even *be* a Scotland today if Isabella hadn't bravely stepped forward to crown Robert king, and sadly, when she was captured, Isabella didn't get any greyhounds. Instead, Edward I locked her up for years *in a cage*, which he hung over the side of a castle wall as a cautionary reminder to the Scottish rebels. The same castle wall, in fact, where he had displayed one of Braveheart's chopped-off arms the year before.

Why is nobody celebrating this long-suffering, forgotten heroine? It's disrespectful. Why didn't our ancestors take the time to record things more completely? And what was it *like* to hang there in a cage next to Braveheart's blue arm for four years? How did Isabella stay alive all that time, out in the elements? Who fed her? Who dealt with her piss pot?

—Kids.

—Please, Mama. We're eating.

Someday this will matter to our children. They may have to deal with the complexity of descending from bigamists and marauding monks, artist-inventors and feuding brothers, heroines and Preserved Fish, and from people who actually enslaved other human beings. They may never truly find out if they're Jewish. But no matter what, they'll have as much as I can piece together for them, because I fervently believe that forgetting is wasteful. The world is a brutal and glorious place. The more we know about what has come before, the more we will know ourselves, and the easier it will be for us, and our children, *and our dogs*, to proceed.

On the subject of Macbeth: a dim bell is ringing. Something about that group of islands off the west coast of Scotland, where all those monks laboriously doodled greyhounds in the margins of manuscripts. Where Macbeth was buried. What was the name of those islands? The Hebrides. There's something else I read about the Hebrides recently—what was it? Something I was researching right before all this family stuff. What was my last big investigation? Wait a second. Ticks?

Oh my gosh. Here it is.

From *Wikipedia*:

Perhaps the first known description of what is now known as Lyme disease appeared in the writings of Reverend Dr. John Walker after a visit to the Island of Jura (Deer Island) off the west coast of Scotland in 1764. He gives a good description of both the symptoms of Lyme disease (with "exquisite pain [in] the interior parts of the limbs") and of the tick vector itself . . . many people from this area of Great Britain immigrated to North America . . . at the end of the 18th century.

—Kids.

—What.

—Your ancestors brought infected ticks to America. They poisoned me.

—*Stop* it, Mama. You're making this up.

13.

Breakthrough

MAY 2012

If anything else happens to him, I will still go to Tokyo. And when I get there, I will kill him.

I try to be on alert when David's working—I scour scripts for the risky scenes, urging caution—but when *Tremé* scheduled a stunt in the final episode of their third season last week, I was totally out of the loop, working in Philadelphia. There's been an interesting Morse household reversal this year, actually: David's had two of the kids down there since last January. Sam finally abandoned New England halfway through sophomore year and is taking a semester off, applying to transfer to a warmer climate and doing an internship in New Orleans. Eliza is living in our rental with them, building a career as a freelance photographer. My first memoir came out last fall, and book events in Philadelphia have caused me to juggle my time between both homes, logging miles with the airline, carefully scheduling coverage for Lilly up north so her life's not too disrupted. So David and I have had a chance to appreciate how the other half lives, David as den mother and me as the traveling partner.

A Lilly breakthrough: After my recovery I began exercising again, often in the evenings, and while the family was home my workout sessions became a useful opportunity for Lilly to practice trusting people besides me. We have a small side room at home with a couple of exercise machines set up in front of a television. This space doubles as Joey's private dining area, and we've always kept the door shut during his mealtime so prowling dogs wouldn't interfere. Lilly accepted my inaccessibility with minimal protest when she had the family for company, and when they all left, I continued my routine of evening exercise sessions, failing to process the fact that Lilly was now essentially *alone, in another room*, sometimes for hours at a time. Because Lilly already understood the routine and knew exactly where I was, she was peaceful when I emerged, sound asleep in the living room.

I still can't believe how long it took me to register the fact that there's an outside entrance to the exercise room. Once this became clear, all it took was some simple adjustments to the security-alarm system. My secret escape hatch has been working for months now, and Lilly has no clue.

It's essential to plan ahead: While Lilly's turned out in the yard, I scurry around doing all the anxiety-inducing things she's identified as my departure cues, gathering purse, shoes, coat, whatever. I stash them near my secret hatch, and then it's a simple acting exercise. I let Lilly in the house and immediately head for the sofa, sighing contentedly, as if there are no plans for the rest of the day. Once she settles, bored, I wander sort of idly into the exercise room. Naturally, Lilly jumps up and tries to follow, but I close the door firmly, just as I would if I were about to work out and Joey's food was vulnerable. I then turn on the TV as usual, stealthily set the alarm (careful not to jangle keys or zip up my jacket), and slither out. Ha!

I can be gone for several hours, and when I return (making sure to come back through the hatch—living in fear I'll blow my cover someday by coming in through the mudroom like a normal person—and, remembering to take off my coat before going out to the living room) Lilly is there, but she's stretching and yawning like an ordinary well-adjusted dog—she's clearly been completely peaceful, positive she had me safely cornered with no means of escape. This technique works for our house sitter Gaillard, too, which is fantastic because now nothing can distract me from going to Tokyo to murder my husband.

David agreed to do a job that will start next week, a miniseries in Japanese, which meant he'd have to fly straight from New Orleans after *Tremé* completed its third season. On his last free day before filming that final stunt in New Orleans, David decided to take a nostalgic bike ride along Lake Pontchartrain, and the ride ended abruptly with a freak crash just around the corner from our house. He's had plenty of bike accidents before, but not quite like this one sounded when he described it to me later on the phone: a sudden dive over the handlebars and a teeth-rattling knock to the head, bad enough to completely, irreparably destroy his helmet and inflict various bumps and scrapes all up and down one side of his body.

—Good lord. Are you okay? Should you see a doctor?

—I'm icing it.

—I hope you're going to let them use a stunt double for that fight.

—Uh . . .

—Come on, David. We're going to Tokyo, it's going to be so much fun! Just this once, let someone else do the frigging stunt.

David likes doing his own stunts, for all sorts of reasons; it's a kick to play cops and robbers, of course, but also he's a stickler for authenticity and a steadfast team player on a film set. More than once he's refused proper medical attention, arriving home in the evening with a broken hand swollen beyond recognition because his character can't be wearing a splint in the scene next morning. His legs are covered with scars from years of being kicked and beaten, and he's down to partial hearing in one ear because he sometimes won't wear earplugs during gunfights (they might show in the close-up). He's been putting off surgery to repair a shoulder and a knee for years now, always squeezing in one more job so as not to disappoint some director.

Acting is a contact sport. Sometimes I feel like I'm married to a professional athlete—we have an entire section of our freezer devoted exclusively to ice packs.

If there'd been more notice, *Tremé* might have been able to dig up a double who looked more like David. The guy they brought in, perfectly capable of handling the stunt (an ugly clash, long overdue, between David's honest cop and an evil coworker) was the right height, but about fifty pounds heavier. So, as I feared, my ~~idiot~~ perfectionist husband decided to do the fight himself. And, as I feared, it was rough.

—*Are you all right?*

—*I'm icing.*

—*Dammit, David. Don't do anything else, please. Lie down and don't move until it's time to go to the airport tomorrow.*

David and I have all these rules about travel. We never fly on the same plane if the kids aren't with us. This doesn't really decrease the odds we'll orphan the children, of course. We drive around in cars together all the time, but flying on separate planes helps me keep my nerves in check during turbulence. David needs quiet time to adjust before starting a big job like this anyway; whenever the kids and I were able to visit during school holidays, I'd always make sure he was settled before we descended. It's been a long time since we've been without the children on location overseas, and out of habit I'd asked the Japanese studio to book my departure from Philly for a few days after David was to leave New Orleans. This gave me a little extra time, and the evening before David was scheduled to depart I was still contemplating my usual checklist of pre-departure errands (*find passport, don't forget anxiety medicine for the long flight and bedside spray bottle for David's Waking-Up Attacks, drop off groceries for Mother Brigid, tell Gaillard about the plumber, pay bills, restock kitty litter and dog food*) when the phone rang: Sam.

—*Don't freak out.*

—*What?*

—*There's something wrong with Papa. The paramedics just took us to some hospital.*

—*WHAT?! What's wrong with him?*

—*They don't know yet, we just got here. He's really dizzy and when he tries to move his face gets all red. He can't stand up.*

—*Okay. Okay. Should I come? I'll come right now. Maybe there's a late flight—*

—*No. Papa says to wait.*

—*He can talk? Can I talk to him?*

—*No, they're running tests. He says to wait. He's okay; he just can't move.*

—*Hold on. Papa's PARALYZED?*

—*No. Mama. It's not THAT bad. I'll call you when we know something.*

—*Okay, but Sam, I'll come in a second if—*

—*I have to go. My phone juice is low and I don't have a charger. That guy Tak from Japan is here and we're waiting. I'll call you.*

—*Oh f3%@! Japan! He knows he's not going, right? Papa can't work if he can't move—*

—*Mama, we don't know anything yet. I've got to go.*

I wandered around in a daze for a few hours, texting Eliza, who happened to be at home for a high school reunion, calling Ben, and hounding Sam to brief the doctors on all David's health issues—the sleep disorder, the allergies, and *this weird thing to do with the blood vessels around his ear; they spotted it years ago and told us to keep an eye on it. Papa might forget, Sam, so ask them if they know about it*—waiting, waiting, until finally the phone rang: David.

—*Oh, thank God. How are you? Do they know what it is?*

—*They aren't saying. They know it wasn't a stroke or a heart attack and I definitely don't have a brain tumor, but I can't stand up, so they're putting me in a room tonight while they figure it out.*

—*Good. So you're not going to Japan.*

—*Not tomorrow.*

—*David. You are having a scary health crisis. You're not going to Japan AT ALL. Right?*

—*Uh . . .*

—*Oh my GOD.*

See? This is what he does.

I could tell immediately what was in play down there. This miniseries (for Japan's public television network, NHK) is a huge undertaking, a period piece starring Ken Watanabe as Yoshida, the Japanese prime minister during the American occupation after World War II. They had gone to a lot of trouble hiring a real American actor to go toe-to-toe with Ken, and David would be playing Gen. Douglas MacArthur, who ran the show after Japan surrendered. NHK has never dealt with our actors' union, so the deal had taken quite a while to settle, making the whole situation extremely last-minute. This producer, Tak, had to Ping-Pong all over the world sorting out David's work visa, delivering it just barely in time.

I'd met Tak on my last trip down there—he's a really nice guy, and now he was probably under tremendous pressure with a tight shooting schedule and skillions of yen or whatever on the line. David must have known that if he backed out, Tak and NHK would be in a terrible jam. And David, as we know, is a team player to the death.

I could have rushed down there and tried handcuffing David to his hospital bed or lying under the wheels of his plane on the tarmac at Louis Armstrong International. But there was no guarantee I'd succeed, and knowing how the SBDs thrive on manipulating the availability of last-minute changes in air travel, I'd probably miss my own flight from Philadelphia to Tokyo, meaning David could end up unconscious in some Japanese trauma center and I'd have no way of getting to him at all. I had to stay put and see how this played out.

I sat in the house all weekend with a phone in my hand and my laptop fixed on the US Airways reservation screen, waiting for texts from Sam, who was valiantly shuttling back and forth between the house and the hospital with his father's special pillows and allergy-free food. (Sam really surprised us. He's one of those still-waters-run-deep types like his father; you can't always tell what's going on in there. As it turns out, he really comes through in a pinch.) By Saturday night, David still couldn't take one step without the world going upside-down. The doctors decided it was a bad case of vertigo, either due to a virus or, more likely, the crystals in David's inner ear had been knocked out of place when he hit his head on that bike ride. Whatever the cause, the ideal way to recover from vertigo is plenty of rest.

—*David, what the f%^&? You're still going?*

—*I should be okay. I walked down the hall by myself today. They gave me motion-sickness pills and steroids, and Tak has organized wheelchair assistance at the airports tomorrow. He says NHK is willing to chance it.*

—*Oh, great! How nice of them. Does your doctor know you have to travel for almost twenty-four hours? And then instead of recovering from jet lag, you'll dive immediately into a month-long job with Japanese people who work like lunatics and never sleep and you're going to insist on working just as hard as them because you are a total nincompoop and definitely going through a midlife crisis and if you are not in a coma already by the time I get there I will immediately find you and put you in one myself and then do the same to everyone in Japan, which sort of defeats the purpose?*

—*Uh . . .*

—*Great. Really, this is so great. See you soon.*

This should not be happening. What kind of wife am I, anyway? I knew this could happen, and I should have stopped it. I should have been down there all winter, but *no*, instead I've been here, swanning around with my memoir, mooning over my rescue dog.

*　　*　　*

So. Kitty litter is stocked and bills are paid. Ma has her groceries, and I am positive I have my passport—I keep rifling inside my purse making sure it's still there.

Gaillard comes over when I'm about to leave; he can tell I'm a wreck.

—Don't worry, Susan. Lilly will be fine.

—Lilly *who?*

And I'm off.

14.

Bookends

We're leery of these toilets.

When you approach the one in our hotel bathroom, the lid lifts automatically. I find this kind of charming; I've been missing Lilly again, and being greeted by our toilet each morning is like waking up to a cheerful new kind of pet.

David, however, feels personally threatened—I think he'd rather make his own choices about the orientation of his toilet lids. He may be messing with this one a little, sending mixed signals, possibly sneaking around the perimeter of the room on entry so as not to trigger the sensors. While he was brushing his teeth last night he says he was distracted by a whirring noise coming from behind. When he turned around, he caught the lid of the john in the act of opening, which he found sort of presumptuous; he'd been in the bathroom for quite a while and had given no indication of any interest in using the toilet. When he tried closing the lid manually, he claims the thing resisted, and somehow during the scuffle it slammed down rather abruptly on his hand, and refused to open.

I'm definitely intimidated by the toilet in David's dressing room at the studio. You have to lift the lid yourself, which after a few days in our posh hotel is a hardship. David's dressing-room toilet compensates for this deficiency with a dizzying array of alternative functions controlled by buttons displayed on a single armrest, helpfully diagrammed and labeled in English.

The Volume feature seems superfluous, as does another marked Spray, which sports a big, rounded ₩ (clearly meant to represent someone's bottom) with a little cartoon fountain ejaculating up at the ₩ from below. I cannot imagine submitting to Spray without a change of clothes handy, so I've been careful not to touch that button. It's tempting, though, given there's no other option that appears remotely likely to persuade this dressing-room toilet to flush, aside from one labeled Flushing Sound (whimsically illustrated with musical notes).

Flushing Sound did not, however, trigger any kind of useful result the first time I tried it. It merely caused the whole appliance to erupt with a lusty, deep-throated *SOOOOUUUUNND*, roaring enthusiastically no matter what I tried, including repeatedly, frantically, jabbing Stop, or (in despair, before fleeing) hammering Volume's minus sign with every last ounce of strength (which I think may have muffled Flushing Sound somewhat, although by then I was too rattled to stick around and find out).

There must be superior logic at play. This is Japan, after all.

I encountered a singularly accommodating toilet in the ladies' room at a fancy restaurant in Tokyo's Ginza District. When I first went in I couldn't find a light switch, and while I was fumbling around in the dark, the seat began to glow eerily—blue, like a nightlight.

When using shared facilities on a Japanese soundstage, you must swap your shoes for special bathroom-only slippers. It's very important to remember to change back before returning to work. More than once, David has been tackled at the men's-room threshold by members of the crew intent on keeping him from contaminating the floor of their set with offensive bathroom microbes.

David's okay with the vertigo, though he might really have to lock up the sharp objects now that I know a few things. Instead of resting after the stunt that day in New Orleans, David went and played frigging *golf* with his cronies from the crew. And get this: the doctor told him she couldn't forbid this trip, but she'd never get on a plane in his condition herself. I'm trying not to think about it too hard—what's done is done. In a way, I'm glad we're here, now that we understand what the real agenda is. Japan is still in recovery from that dreadful tsunami, and the financial crisis has affected everyone deeply. They're in need of a morale booster, and NHK has figured out that a vivid reminder of the story of their survival after the devastating humiliation of World War II could be inspiring.

We've always wanted to come back to Japan. We tend to hold out until work takes us to faraway places like this, when travel and lodging is covered, which means when we do go somewhere distant and exotic there are all sorts of time restraints. We were disappointed by our first visit—a quick, wasted Tokyo pit stop on the way home after a long job David had in New Zealand and Thailand. What babies we were. I was pregnant with Eliza; we were eager to get home and could not manage much more than a stifling bus crawl from the airport to overpriced hotel sushi, a sprint past the Imperial Palace, and a tourist-trap shiatsu massage.

I've always had a feeling we'd come back, because there seems to be a mutual attraction going between David and all things Japanese. David's best dining option allergy-wise is sushi, and I think he acquired a sort of fan base here at some point. He had a flurry of very entertaining letters from some ardent ladies in Japan back in the 1990s, mostly incoherent due to the language barrier, and he was actually sort of chased once, Beatles-style, by a squealing pack of Japanese schoolgirls on a field trip when they spotted him window-shopping in Cambridge, England. Usually people are sort of confused when they recognize David—they can't figure out why they know his face, and assume he went to high school with them or something. Those Japanese girls in Cambridge knew exactly who David was.

I'm waiting to identify the significance, if there is any—wondering why our first faraway trip together as empty nesters brings us back to the setting of that final, botched fling on the brink of parenthood. Now, a quarter of a century later, just a month shy of our thirtieth wedding anniversary, we're in Tokyo again, only a little worse for wear.

Actually, David looks better than I expected. The steroids seem to be helping. The people at NHK are being incredibly hospitable, bending over backward to make sure he's comfortable and well fed, eager to show me around and help find what we need to keep things running smoothly. At first I stuck close to David, keeping an eye on him while fighting jet lag on the dressing-room sofa during the day. Now that I'm confident they are not going to kill him, I've been indulging in adventures. A friendly young Canadian actor named Eric took me on the subway to see his stomping grounds in the Kabukichō District, where I got a peek at Tokyo nightlife—fascinating—long-haired, skinny David Cassidy types dressed in skintight black suits and cartoonish, pointy-toed shoes straight out of *The Mikado*, loitering on street corners distributing pamphlets for the "host bars."

Host bars are not about sex. You can find legal sex for hire here, but Eric says a lot of single Japanese professional women are lonely, and too busy to organize a social life. They don't want to cook after work, and they are practically phobic about eating alone in a restaurant, so the hosts are in great demand just for dinner and conversation at the end of a lengthy workday. Why any woman would prefer to eat with these androgynous boy-band types I'm not sure, but the female customers have their own rather baffling style: ankle socks with patent-leather party shoes, pigtails, and schoolgirl kilts are the rage for these young twentysomethings out on the town.

It's a little like New Orleans, in fact, all these costumes, but the biggest surprise so far has been the dogs in Tokyo's tony shopping district, Ginza: A pug, sporting a leather vest and chaps. Pairs of poodles in pink-and-purple tutus. A Weimaraner dressed as a farmer—plaid flannel shirt and denim overalls with a handy functional slit at the business end.

I'm aware of recent dog trends in Manhattan—tiny Chihuahuas peeking out of designer purses—but clearly Japanese people are taking things further. Inexplicably, a lot of them like to push their full-sized dogs, really big ones, around in baby strollers. Nobody has been able to explain the point of this, but I swear it's true. The sight of it almost comforts me—I feel a little less foolish about fussing over Lilly with coats and special beds.

This is the longest I've been away from Lilly since she arrived, and I feel like an amputee with phantom-limb syndrome. I keep thinking it's time to go for a walk, even though I know Gaillard's got it covered, sending me e-mails to ease my withdrawal—reassuring photographs of Lilly and Joey lolling together on our lawn in the sunshine.

Big news: I've finally gotten to the bottom of Flushing Sound. Eric says Japanese women are bashful; they don't like anyone to hear what they're doing in public facilities, so they flush the toilets over and over while they're engaged. Overflushing is a serious concern in this island country due to a water shortage (especially since the recent earthquake), and the quick fix for ladies' public toilets has been Flushing Sound. Apparently there are endless options I have yet to experience—heated massage seats, toilets that play classical music, toilets equipped with air deodorizers and little blow driers so there's no need for mopping up after employing the Spray function. I hear foreign visitors grow so attached they arrange to take particular favorites home with them.

We will not be importing a souvenir toilet.

I am trying not to think too much about David's most recent report from the bathroom in our hotel apartment. Sometimes when he's sitting down, he hears a subtle mechanical noise coming from somewhere deep inside our john, which (he insists) signals the emergence of a skinny metal probe-type tube, inspecting him from below. I fervently dread a midnight encounter with David's probe.

But the toilet's not the only thing that confuses us in this apartment, which is very comfortable despite a random beeping noise I can't identify. I think it's either the laundry machine or the dishwasher. Plus, I cannot for the life of me figure out how to work the television. I had to spend some time working alone in here the other day, and there was an actual earth tremor, my first since our big one in 1994. David thinks this building is probably earthquake-proof, but still, the whole country is a seismic powder keg after all, and that one little shake flashed me right back to our patio with the ceramic tiles raining down. I spent the next hour or so cowering in a fetal position on the floor by our bed, feeling rather foolish, especially because the people down at the front desk did not seem even slightly rattled.

They're prepared in this city. Eric says Tokyo soda vending machines are programmed to dispense their wares for free if there's a big earthquake. He was in town for the horrible one last year, the one that caused the tsunami. Eric makes his bread and butter in "stop-motion" as a body double for animated martial-arts-type video games, and he was working that day, on a very high floor of a building in one of the business districts where everything's pretty much earthquake-proofed. He has no children, and he was not particularly scared when the shaking began, partly because he could see out the window into a tall building across the street, where there was a guy at his desk rocking from one foot to another as his own building swayed, still typing away at his computer.

It's true the workers in Tokyo never stop. I'm very grateful the Screen Actors' Guild rules restricted David from submitting to the typical Japanese actor's twenty-hour workday, although he has compromised, allowing much shorter turnarounds than he's used to. He's coped pretty well, considering, not exactly pacing himself, but I think he'll survive. And now, finally, he has a few days off before going into the countryside next week to film an outdoor scene: MacArthur's iconic arrival after the surrender, poised triumphantly on the aircraft's top step, brandishing his signature corncob pipe. (MacArthur was a showman. David's been studying old newsreels, and he's supposed to *jog* down those steps, which may be a challenge.)

Our NHK friends graciously arranged a real treat to kick off our holiday: tickets to one of the final days of the big Grand Sumo Tournament. A famous Hawaiian Sumo champ named Konishiki kindly offered his box at the stadium, which was amazing. It's like being given priceless, unattainable Super Bowl tickets—a huge thrill for our companions (David's translator, Yoshi, and Tadashi, the line producer for the miniseries), both avid Sumo aficionados.

It was very odd seeing something like this without the kids. Till now, I've always had them with me for the big trips. Sumo is just the sort of thing the boys would love, and I kept identifying photo opportunities for Eliza. So much pageantry—kimono-clad officials dancing around, striking brass gongs and chanting; the gigantic elaborately ponytailed wrestlers strutting in, adjusting their fancy, tasseled silk thongs, tossing handfuls of coarse salt (a Shinto ritual meant to purify the ring before each bout), gravely bowing, repeatedly slapping their massive rippling flanks in preparation, then squatting in astonishing deep pliés, impossibly nimble and flexible for their size. Sumo wrestlers live together, almost monastically, in communal "training stables." (Like racing dogs!) There's none of the brutality of an American boxing match; Sumo is as quick as a thirty-second dog race, the only objective being to force one's opponent out of the ring or onto the floor, either of which can happen in a flash, at which point the winner helps the loser up (if necessary) and they bow all over again. Brilliant.

Next: a night in historic Kyoto; train tickets and hotel carefully organized by our gracious Japanese hosts. Everyone's hyperaware that we have to keep David intact for MacArthur's jog down the airplane steps. With the help of an extremely efficient guide, Hiro, we've covered a lot—palaces and museums, temples and shrines. For lunch: skimmed tofu, a slippery experience, which will sound utterly disgusting if I try to describe it, but in fact was delectable.

Romance is everywhere. As the story goes, Kyoto was removed from a short list of targets for the second atom bomb in World War II because the American secretary of war once honeymooned here. I love seeing real working geisha dressed in traditional kimonos, trotting briskly to liaisons along narrow cobblestone streets. We're trotting briskly ourselves—me hovering behind David in case he topples unexpectedly, both of us conscious of the role reversal between this and our first tour of New Orleans, when I was the fragile one—so much to see, torn, wanting to cover everything and savor details: creaking "nightingale floors" at a palace, designed to alert the shogun when enemies approached; a precarious jumble of turtles piled on a small rock behind a Shinto shrine; a stepping-stone bridge surrounded by water lilies. Just before we cross, something strikes me: A need to stop and document this sweet, fleeting adventure at the close of our thirtieth year. Impulsively, I toss the camera to Hiro and take David's hand.

Back in Tokyo, our neglected toilet yawns reproachfully. David has left his special allergy-free toothpaste behind in Kyoto, the stores are closed tonight, and when I finally manage to turn on the complicated BlackBerry NHK loaned me, it's jammed with a series of text messages, forwarded somehow from my American cell phone: Mother Brigid's in the *hospital*?

I did try to set up a plan before leaving in case something like this happened. Colette is already on it in England, talking on the phone to nurses *(Don't worry, Sizzle, she tripped on the way to the bathroom, just a little break, no surgery. Everything will be fine)*, Gaillard has looked in on her already *(Don't worry, Susan, I left by the exercise room while Lilly was sleeping. Everything will be fine)*, and the best news for Ma is some of her priests are in town *(Mother Brigid says don't worry, Susie; we've blessed her. Everything will be fine)*.

So. I guess everything will be fine. No sense in calling; they're all fast asleep. A familiar weightless sensation washes over me again, the feeling I had when Sam took care of his father earlier this month.

Transferring the Kyoto pictures to my laptop, I pause. This moment at the pond, when I'd tossed Hiro the camera and took David's hand—it's familiar. I scroll through my files, searching among scanned pictures from the dawn of time. I know what I'm looking for.

Hiro told us stepping-stones are a meaningful feature of a Zen garden, symbolic of the Way, the spiritual journey through life. They force us to slow down, enjoy the sights, appreciate the dangers, and live each moment in the now instead of focusing on some imagined destination. This, I now see, is what we've been trying to do all these decades—navigating births and earthquakes, health crises and rogue toilets, doing our best to stop when we can to savor the scenery, and contemplate the murky depths with respect. Even if we don't know where we're going, we can always take time to see where we are.

Found it. A visual haiku. Perfect bookends.

Lying Dragon Bridge, 2012

Grand Palace, 1988

15.

Front-Hall Bridge

They're doing it again.

She's rolling around on the bed, saying, "I'm coming, David, I'm coming, wait, where is it, oh, oh, oh, wait I'm coming!" *And he's saying,* "EL. E. EL. O. EL. E. ELLLLL."

It's very dark in here, which means this is not breakfast time and you should stay.

She drops everything on the floor and says, "Darn! Where is it? Here!" *And he says,* "ELL," *and she says,* "I'm spritzing, David, I'm spritzing, don't you feel it?" *And he says,* "ELLLLL!!!" *and she says,* "Rats. Hang on, let me think of something else."

*   *   *

I'm learning to expect the unexpected. Back in Hell's Kitchen in the 1980s, if you'd told me the bohemian actor I'd fallen for would eventually want to move with me to my upper-crusty birthplace and take up golf, I'd have said, *David? In a polo shirt? Out on the driving range comparing handicaps with Addison J. Waspington III? Never.* And then, if you'd told me I'd voluntarily spend every second of my own spare time seated at a card table—*Me? Playing bridge? Nibbling cocktail nuts?*— I'd have laughed in your face.

This is my friend Ellen's fault—she tricked me. She knows I'm not the garden-club type, but she also knows I'm a compulsive puzzler. Plus, she knows we have an empty nest most of the year now. *It's what we're all going to be doing when our children are gone, when we're too old to do anything but sit.* I thought, *Not me,* but I agreed to step in one time when they needed a fourth, strictly out of curiosity, and now I can't stop.

It's a sickness, and the three ABBA ladies I play with are my codependents. We're mostly at Courtney's—I steer us there as often as possible because Courtney has no cats or tiny edible dogs, meaning greyhounds are welcome, and Lilly's friendly with Courtney's two Labradors, Maggie and Milo. We walk our dogs together in the woods—Lilly dainty on the leash; Courtney hollering at Maggie and Milo, who like to barrel ahead tracking down filthy discarded soda cans and castoff condoms.

Courtney's from Nashville, a survivor on two levels—first of a haphazard, eccentric *Glass Castle*-style upbringing, and recently of breast cancer. She's a skilled architect—not for hire now, because her husband provides well and she's been raising three athletically intimidating kids. Courtney channels her creativity into their ranch in Idaho and her home around the corner from my place: a 1912 Arts and Crafts with a front hall to die for, the size of a small ballroom, looking out on the garden, easily accommodating two fabulous craftsman-type bridge tables.

Bridge is a four-person card game played by opposing sets of paired players. Courtney's most frequent partner is my Drayton cousin Ruthie—another survivor. Over a decade ago, Ruthie's beloved brother committed suicide (depression) at age forty-three, leaving behind a fine wife and three young daughters. Then, less than two years later, Ruthie's father died of dementia. So Ruthie's been holding the family together. She has three kids, including one math whiz about to graduate from a top university, and another Ivy contender currently entering his crucial senior year in high school wearing an elaborate, scary-looking brace from neck to waist— three fractured vertebrae—following a near-tragic accident, a dive off a pier into shallow water on Martha's Vineyard last July. Ruthie's maiden name is Strong, and she has earned it. She's our most advanced player, devastatingly quick-witted, and a stickler for propriety.

We all worry Ruthie may abandon us—she's had formal bridge lessons and we've been taking a while to catch up to her level. Plus, her partner, Courtney, is only playing for laughs. Meaning Courtney blatantly cheats, shamelessly bombarding Ruthie with an illegal fusillade of throat clearing, obvious hand signals, and facial tics during the crucial bidding phase of our games when the goal is to communicate as much as possible to your partner without flat-out telling her what's in your hand.

Courtney's illegal signaling makes me crazy. I tend to scream and curse a lot when we play, even though (I probably shouldn't admit this) my partner Ellen and I have our own scam going. Ellen is a tad psychic, and I think she pretty much knows everything about my hand before I've picked up my cards. Ellen's the only one of us with an actual day job—she's been using her considerable social skills as the alumni fund-raiser for a local school for years now. I think Ellen's focused intently on bridge these days because she wants to stop working soon to be with her husband, who's working a lot in New York, but she's mainly in it for the fun (like Courtney) and because (like Ruthie) her father died of dementia and she wants to keep her mental muscle in shape in case of any lurking tendency in her genes. Ellen's a compulsive puzzler like me, wickedly competitive but naturally adept at peacekeeping, knowing instinctively when to break the tension with a deftly placed wisecrack.

The first time we played, Lilly had a hard time settling down because of all the screams and laughter. Now she makes herself at home, cheerfully fending off attention from Maggie and Milo, and reclining decorously by my chair on the designer carpet in Courtney's front hall, which suits her.

Courtney keeps marveling lately at how much Lilly's adjusted in the last two years. She really has unfolded, just like a flower. She knows our routine and loves it. I first noticed the change last June, after Japan. As is our custom, we left Asia on separate flights, not just as a precaution but because David's car was still in New Orleans and he had to pack up the rental house before driving north for the summer. Lilly always sticks even closer to me for a while when I'm back from a trip. As usual, she dogged me around the house the first few days, and she was only just beginning to trust me out of her sight by the evening David was due to arrive home.

Lilly was on her favorite bed in the living room, asleep, when David's car pulled into the driveway. I was in the kitchen putting dishes away when I heard his key at the door, and before I even processed what was happening, Lilly came bounding in from the living room, *grinning*, pushing past me to sniff David's suitcase and shoes, insisting on having her ears rubbed in that special David way, the way she *likes* it, prancing across the driveway with him for more bags, wanting to assist, her tail high like a flag. When he finally sat at the kitchen table to look through his mail, Lilly was still there, fleetingly resting her needle nose on his knee, politely claiming his attention, and then, catching herself, careful not to overstep, regretfully turning to trot out of the room to her bed.

David and I sat together holding our breath for a few beats, marveling, and suddenly, as if she just couldn't help herself, back Lilly came to sniff one more time, and flop at his feet with a sigh. *He belongs. He is ours.*

That's when I knew: Lilly has found her true Forever Home.

Here's the kicker: Linda O'Brien discovered a website where you can plug in your greyhound's official racing name and get a much more complete record of racing results. I knew Lilly had competed for a few seasons and even had a couple of wins, but the printout I was given when we adopted her had some odd, longish gaps. I'd always wondered darkly if the gaps were due to her injuries—those scars—the deep one on her front shoulder, that shredded ear.

When I plugged Lilly's formal racing name into the site Linda found, it turned out our shrinking violet was practically a star. Lilly raced uninterrupted for over two years: more than a hundred starts with a total of fifteen wins. The figures include brief notes describing the nature of the dog's performance in a given race. Some are harrowing—*Fell first turn; Hit*—but my favorite note is for a race Lilly ran one February in Texas: *Flew to wire inside*. Flew! That's our Lilly (as if we'd had anything to do with it). Then, using the new information, I found actual videos of her last few wins in Florida, and we saw Lilly in her glory, running, bursting out of the gate, flying around the track with abandon, lengths ahead of the pack—magnificent.

Googling greyhound races is not for the faint of heart. Inevitably, you wind up watching videos of accidents—dogs tumbling head over heels, shattering those lovely, delicate limbs, lying still on the track in crumpled heaps. The inner rail that runs the lure they chase is electrified, and dogs have been literally fried on the spot when they cut a turn too close. There are all kinds of horrifying stories: track dogs found with cocaine in their systems, presumably to make them run faster; greyhounds riddled with parasites, stacked in crates for years, turned out only a few times each day, dying of heatstroke while racing in hundred-degree temperatures; then sold for medical research, or disposed of in sickening ways. There's disagreement in the rescue community about whether or not this kind of abuse is still unchecked. Some experts say conditions are much better in the US now, and I hope that's true. The worst crimes seem to take place in Spain, where dogs are being starved, hanged, decapitated, and everywhere photos of pile after pile of emaciated greyhound bodies.

People who have devoted their lives to rescue have a reputation for fanaticism. When you really think about what they've been rescuing these dogs from, you understand. It's shocking and inconceivable, and somehow knowing the risk Lilly took each time she raced distinguishes her triumphs even further. Whether striding bravely or creeping tentatively toward unavoidable new challenges as she ages, like all the ABBA ladies and friends I admire, Lilly is with us in that darkened *Toy Story* movie theater, our throats catching as Woody and the gang grasp hands, paws, and trotters on their way down the chute. Lilly, with all her quirks and hang-ups, is one of our heroes, an exquisite force. A survivor.

Things are really good right now. Both boys are back in college— Ben still in Texas and Sam has officially transferred down south. David's on another summer hiatus from *Tremé*, filming at home for a change. Eliza's up from New Orleans for the month, hired to take stills on the independent movie David's doing, so they're having fun together. After a brief incarceration in the skilled nursing wing arranged by Colette while I was in Japan, Mother Brigid's in fine form as well—working on her iPad skills, which, while not perfect, are pretty good for a ninety-year-old:

From: Mother Brigid

Date: Sept 18, 2012 2:45 pm

To: Susan Morse

Subject: Autumn Colors

Live as we are meant to do. Every blazing leaf is a sign of who is in charge.

In our Saviour's love the only Friend of MAn, unworthy nun,pilgrimess, Ma.

Sent from my iPad

I can't help my tendency to mistrust happy times, though.

—Ma. This e-mail of yours about who's in charge. I have a question.

—Yes?

—I feel like we keep having one calamity after another. I know we're blessed and everything; things are basically good, relatively speaking. But I don't understand why I'm constantly putting out fires—earthquakes, health crises, whatever—I think I'm supposed to be learning something and I'm not grasping what it is.

—Oh. No. Those are the demons doing that. You're under attack. We all are, always, and the best thing to do is say our prayers.

—The Show Business Demons? When did I tell you about the SBDs?

—The what?

—Never mind. Yes. Thanks, Ma. Demons. I'll say my prayers.

The phone rang while I was exercising this morning. It was almost a relief, a chance to let off some steam.

—*Hello?*

—*Cracklecracklecracklecrack.*

—*Yes?*

—*Cracklecracklecracklecrack.*

—*If this is a robo-call I'm hanging up.*

—*Cracklecra—*

—*Okay. Here I go, I'm hanging—*

—*CrackleRe-ports of shots fired near insert lo-cation here. Crackle.*

—*Excuse me?*

—*CracklePolice are re-sponding. Crackle. Remain in-side slash seek shel-ter immediately. Cra—*

—*What? Wait,* what*? Police?! SHOTS FIRED?!*

—*CrackleUpdates to foll-ow. Cra—*

—*Shots fired* where*? Hello? HELLO?!*

—*Click.*

I peered out the window, feeling both frantic and foolish, seeing no SWAT team in our immediate vicinity. I tried CNN: nothing. But clearly something was up —wait, didn't I sign up for incident alerts with Ben's and Sam's colleges? While I was still paralyzed, trying to decide which boy to call first, our phone rang again. I picked up immediately, the familiar static sending a jolt of adrenaline up my spine.

—*Hello?*

—*Cracklecracklecrack. Please dis-regard message shooter. CrackleIt was sent in err-or. CrackleThere is no shooting event on cam-pus. Crackle.*

—*Click.*

Technology is such a marvel.

I've been meaning to visit the boys anyway. One of the perks of the empty nest is you can go see them in their new element, meet their friends, take everyone out for a nice meal, and generally spoil them. If I get right on it, I can spend a night each in Texas and Louisiana and be home before anyone realizes I'm gone. There's not really any work to do this week, so I book my hotels, arrange a stay for Lilly with the O'Briens (David, Eliza, and Gaillard will be gone most days), cancel all bridge games, and head to the airport.

Settled in my seat waiting for takeoff to Austin, I have a sinking realization I've forgotten something crucial: my flight-anxiety pills. My crutch. Ever since that hysterical trip fifteen years ago when I panicked in turbulence worrying about how the family would cope if I died, blubbering my rosary on the in-flight phone with my mother, I have never once dared fly without them.

And of course it's a bumpy one. I could have ordered a drink, something strong, but the flight's too short; I'm picking up a rental car in Texas and I don't want to drive under the influence. I really mustn't make a scene on this plane—there's a woman sitting next to me, and her two small, impressionable children are right across the aisle. They do not need to see some strange lady have a conniption. Nothing to do but sit here quietly, and, as Mother Brigid advises, say my prayers.

It really is pretty bumpy. With each lurch the children across the aisle yelp and giggle. I actually manage to smile at them, or at least flash gritted teeth in their general direction (alternately muttering prayers under my breath, trying to distract myself with a Sudoku book I picked up at the airport kiosk), thinking back to 1998, a flight to L.A. to visit David on *The Green Mile:* pint-sized Sam, Ben, and Eliza in a row, absorbed in their Gameboys, oblivious to the danger, to the orphaned future I wanted so desperately to spare them. When we finally land in Texas I'm pathetically proud of myself for keeping it together.

It's lovely seeing Ben. He's in a studio apartment off campus, living alone this year, and I'm pleased to see how tidy he keeps it.

We have a fun day visiting gardens and the LBJ presidential library. Austin's surprisingly progressive for a Texas capital—they're having a Gay Pride parade, of all things, outside my hotel after dinner. So I'm happy, ready for my next challenge: the flight to New Orleans, cold turkey again.

This time my neighbor is a fellow who wants to chat. There's no turbulence, so I decide to tell him about the breakthrough I'm having, partly because I'm so impressed with myself and partly to warn him in case I go unexpectedly bonkers midflight. *Not to worry,* he says. He's a music manager visiting a client in New Orleans, a singer, and he flies all the time, so he's seen everything. In fact, on his last flight this man started to freak out while they were taxiing—claustrophobia, he thinks—and they had to stop the plane on the tarmac and let the poor guy off.

I can't explain why I find this conversation comforting. I guess I'm in a sort of celebratory mood—I can fly without meds! Praise the Lord!

David has kept the house in New Orleans between seasons of *Tremé*. This is handy because Eliza can stay there, saving some money while she establishes herself, and Sam is still on the waiting list for a dorm room. He's been sleeping downstairs on the sofa, getting over a cold, and the place is in a bit of disarray after the annual end-of-summer Gulf Coast hurricane. Sam and Eliza evacuated together to friends in Atlanta, and the power was still out when they returned, so there are candles and battery-operated lanterns all over the place, and the porch is filthy with dried mud washed up in the storm. Sam seems glad to see me but behind in work, juggling school and a screenplay he's writing with a friend, with no time for more than a quick bite at the neighborhood deli. We discuss plans to send him for a concert weekend with Ben in Austin next month when the boys turn twenty-one, and I make myself useful picking the house up a little for David's eventual return.

Like I said, things are good. There is something amazing and wonderful about visiting your children out in their worlds, watching them find their sea legs as adults.

It's not till my third and final drug-free flight heading home that I figure it out. I know why I don't need those meds anymore—my job is basically done. My children are perfectly capable of moving forward without me at this point, Mother Brigid is squared away, and David will definitely survive whatever happens. It is finally safe for me to relax. Anything from this moment forth is purely for my own enjoyment.

And the powerful, intangible empathy I've felt for Lilly comes into focus. It's no accident I've been so distracted by a dog with anxiety issues—we're one and the same, Lilly and me. As with me, the most demanding part of Lilly's life is past. We've both left the treadmill behind us, and now here we are, two strong females keeping it together in our own ways, temporarily hampered, weakened—justifiably, perhaps—by an Achilles' heel–type tendency to fret excessively about the future.

Maybe Ma's right. Maybe it's all about prayer. Who knows?

Maybe we'll find out someday. But what I do know is that with time and persistence, you can weather the storm, emerge, set goals, and maybe, if you're lucky, as Betty Friedan has assured us, you'll enjoy whatever comes next.

You might even win at bridge.

We're seated around Courtney's hall table in the final throes of a death match. It's been particularly rowdy this morning. The serious bridge veterans we've seen (there's a whole gang of hardcore dragons ruling the country club) are deadly quiet when they play—banter is completely taboo, not just because someone might illegally signal their partner (*ahem*, Courtney). Extraneous noise is extremely distracting in bridge because you win by remembering what cards have been played. Our group would be banned immediately from any grown-up tournament—we can't ever seem to shut up. Right now everyone's screaming at once. Ellen has pulled a last-minute surprise, trumping an ace Courtney was secretly hoarding, and nobody can agree on who actually won because we've forgotten which of us took the previous trick.

Ruthie likes to keep us moving:

—Susan, it's your deal. Courtney, get hold of yourself. We are now going to beat them until they cry.

I deal. Ellen, who's been having terrible hot flashes all summer, peels off her fleece.

—Why does it still feel like August? I can't believe I have to go in today. There's no AC in my office. It's *miserable*.

I look up, surprised.

—Ellen, I thought you quit! When's your official last day?

Ominous silence. Ellen doesn't respond, and I could swear she's sending me urgent psychic danger signals. I stop dealing, alarmed. Courtney has nothing to say for once, her eyes like saucers. Ruthie is staring straight ahead, erect and poker-faced. My heart sinks.

—Oh no! Was I not supposed to say anything?

Nervous, tension-breaking laughter erupts from everywhere. Apparently I've gotten it wrong. Ellen's been a huge asset as the school's alumni fund-raiser; they'll have a hard time filling her shoes when she goes, and besides, she's not retiring, she's just cutting back her hours so she can travel more with her busy husband. I've been so out of the loop in our tiny school community since the kids graduated, I've lost my sensitivity to how swiftly combustible news like this can fly out of control. These women are fast friends, they're deeply protective of one another, but the bottom line is that Courtney, with her notoriously uncontrollable mouth, is not meant to know Ellen's news yet.

Everyone swears secrecy and we go back to our screaming death match, arguing over the conventions, accidentally skipping people's turns, fumbling cards, Ellen calling Ruthie *a female dog* when Ruthie deftly snags a crucial trick, Courtney accusing Lilly of farting, me accusing Courtney of blaming her own digestive troubles on my innocent, perfect dog. All the while I'm openly kicking myself for blowing Ellen's cover. I cannot for the life of me remember being told her news was a secret.

Ellen kindly reassures me.

—Don't worry, it's fine. Now we all know we'll be playing more bridge!

This is a game that sharpens one's mind, but the trick is you need to have a mind capable of being sharpened in the first place. Menopause is a slippery slope, and it's highly likely all four of us may have lost our chance to keep things properly oiled in the memory department.

Walking the dogs later, Courtney tells me I didn't actually spill the beans. She and Ruthie have known for weeks—Ellen has forgotten she gave them both the news herself, it seems, and, loving Ellen, sensing her vulnerability during a big life transition, Courtney doesn't want to rub Ellen's nose in her own faulty recollection of what she's told whom. Courtney's bigmouth reputation doesn't bother her in the slightest anyway, and she commiserates with me generously.

—I can keep a secret. Ruthie always says it's the people I *tell* who can't.

And with a wink, she's off after Milo and Maggie, trespassing down our friend Rose's driveway toward the henhouse.

—Hey, DOGS! I have TREATS! Get away from those chickens!

I watch Courtney go. She can really move when she wants to—you'd never know the doctors took both pairs of ovaries and breasts and pumped her with poison for months.

Lilly and I wait in the quiet street, admiring fall colors. This is middle age. I have the feeling if we ABBA ladies can keep cutting ourselves a little slack, all will be well. In fact, it's looking like it might turn out to be a blast.

Just lie here. If you don't move, they'll stop so you can go back to sleep.

She says, "I'm spritzing, I'm spritzing!" *And he says,* "ELLLLLLLLLL" *and she says,* "S^&#. Okay, David I'm going to try something new. Get ready. Are you ready? Here goes," *and she says,* "YAAAAAAAAAAAAAAAAAAAAH!"

And it hurts your ears, so you jump up and he jumps up and she jumps up and says, "Sorry. The spray bottle didn't work, and I had to surprise you. Are you okay?"

"Thank you," *he says.*

"I'm so sorry," *she says.* "I couldn't think what to do. I was desperate, so I screamed. Are you all right?"

"I'm okay," *he says.* "Except that my ears are ringing a bit."

"I love you," *she says.*

"I love you too," *he says.*

He lies back down. She lies back down.

It's dark.

"He's all right now, Lilly," *she whispers.* "We can go back to sleep."

You lie back down.

It's quiet now. Maybe it's breakfast time soon.

You love them too.

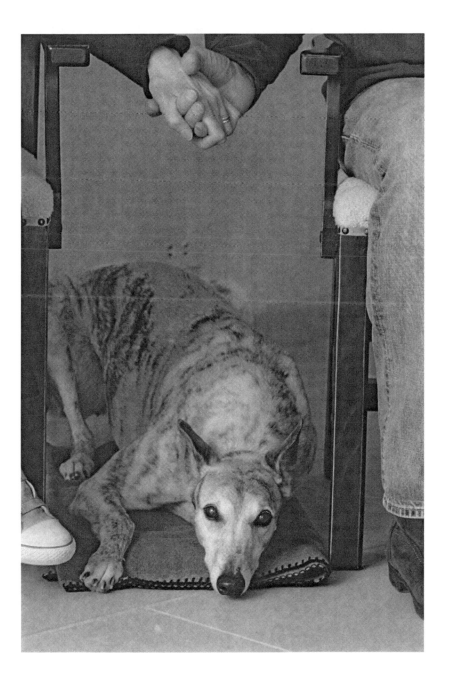

A Note on Greyhound Adoption

No question: I'd adopt another greyhound in a heartbeat. Not just because these gifted dogs have been exploited too long by a multimillion-dollar industry. Not just because the three-hundred-plus volunteer groups in the United States and Canada are working around the clock to find homes for tens of thousands of dogs coming off the track every year. Not just because too many of these beautiful animals have not made it to rescue, dying in miserable obscurity.

I'll adopt again because I can't help myself. Greyhounds are simply so heart-stoppingly wonderful: loyal, gentle, smart, graceful, clean, quiet, funny, and, of course—*fast*. (Come to think of it, maybe that's what this has been about for me all along: my personal solution to the classic midlife craving for a sports car? I don't have to *drive* fast, I can just watch Lilly run mad, goofy forty-mile-an-hour figure eights around my yard.)

The Greyhound Project (adopt-a-greyhound.org) will direct prospective greyhound lovers to their local adoption groups, and many more resources are out there. Join in!

Acknowledgments

Thanks to the dog people: my personal mainstay Linda O'Brien and her boys Richard, Dylan, and King; training experts Deb Lipartito and Ruth Anne Cionca; and to the saints in the trenches—Claudia Presto of Greyhound Gang, Cynthia Branigan of Make Peace With Animals, John Pastor at Philadelphia Animal Welfare Society, and Lisa Fontalbert and Marilyn Varnberg of Greyhound Adoptions of Florida.

To generous friends who answered many questions: Susan Burch; Robin and Lucien Calhoun; Francesca Dalglish; Pamela Dunlap; Ruthie Ferraro; Diane Fleming; Ellen Gray; Ellen Hass; Courtney Kapp; Anne, Jim, and Ben McCormick; Lisa K. Miller; Tricia Nalle; and Barbara Ziv. And to thoughtful readers

Virginia Ingr, Peter Riva, Diane Golden, and my two-for-two title man, Michael Bamberger.

To the Open Road wizards: Jane Friedman, Jeff Sharp, Rachel Chou, Nicole Passage, Chris Davis, Mary McAveney, Allison Underwood, Rachel Krupitsky, Andrea Worthington, and fellow dog-lover Tina Pohlman, who divined exactly what this book should be, and made it happen.

To brilliant editor and friend Marjorie Braman—it's been a delight to work with you again.

And to my family: David, Eliza, Ben, and Sam, who live our story and mercifully tolerate the liberties I take; to Lilly, Joey, Arrow, Marbles, and Aya for being perfect; to Mother Brigid for always allowing my jokes with grace; and to Colette—for the rabbit.

Photo Credits

Page 9	Conleth Hill
Page 41	Colette Barrere
Pages 47, 108, and 138	David Morse
Page 167	Linda O'Brien
Page 175	David Morse
Page 191, top	Eliza Morse
Pages 232 and 245	Courtney Kapp

About the Author

Susan Morse was educated at Williams College. She has worked as an actress in L.A. and New York and is the author of *The Habit*. She now lives in Philadelphia with her husband, David, and their three children, when they're home from college.

EBOOKS BY SUSAN MORSE

FROM OPEN ROAD MEDIA

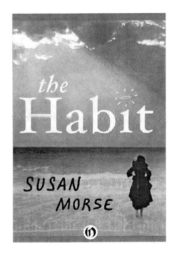

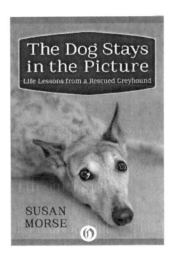

Available wherever ebooks are sold

OPEN ROAD

INTEGRATED MEDIA

Open Road Integrated Media is a digital publisher and multimedia content company. Open Road creates connections between authors and their audiences by marketing its ebooks through a new proprietary online platform, which uses premium video content and social media.

CPSIA information can be obtained at www.ICGtesting.com
Printed in the USA
BVOW07s2004010914

365065BV00001BA/1/P

9 781497 643932